ON JUNETEENTH

· ON ·
JUNETEENTH

Annette Gordon-Reed

LIVERIGHT PUBLISHING CORPORATION

A Division of W. W. Norton & Company

Independent Publishers Since 1923

NEW YORK · LONDON

Frontispiece: Schönberg & Co., Schönberg's Map of Texas (New York: Schönberg & Co, 1866), https://www.loc.gov/item/2002622346/.

For information about permission to reproduce selections from this book,
write to Permissions, Liveright Publishing Corporation,
a division of W. W. Norton & Company, Inc.,
500 Fifth Avenue, New York, NY 10110

For information about special discounts for bulk purchases,
please contact W. W. Norton Special Sales at
specialsales@wwnorton.com or 800-233-4830

"Giant (This Then Is Texas)," words by Paul Francis Webster, music by
Dimitri Tiomkin. Copyright © 1956 (renewed) WC Music Corp.
All rights reserved. Used by permission of Alfred Music.

Manufacturing by Lake Book Manufacturing
Book design by Ellen Cipriano
Production manager: Lauren Abbate

ISBN 978-1-63149-883-1

Liveright Publishing Corporation, 500 Fifth Avenue, New York, N.Y. 10110
www.wwnorton.com

W. W. Norton & Company Ltd., 15 Carlisle Street, London W1D 3BS

1 2 3 4 5 6 7 8 9 0

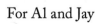

For Al and Jay

CONTENTS

PREFACE

To my surprise some years back, I began to hear people outside of my home state, Texas, talk about, *and actually celebrate* the holiday "Juneteenth." June 19, 1865, shortened to "Juneteenth," was the day that enslaved African Americans in Texas were told that slavery had ended, two years after the Emancipation Proclamation had been signed, and just over two months after Confederate General Robert E. Lee had surrendered to Ulysses S. Grant at Appomattox. Despite the formal surrender, the Confederate army had continued to fight on in Texas until mid-May. It was only after they finally surrendered that Major General Gordon Granger, while at his headquarters in Galveston, prepared General Order Number 3, announcing the end of legalized slavery in the state. The truth is, I confess here, that I was initially annoyed, at least mildly so, when I first heard that others outside of Texas claimed the holiday. But why? After all, it was a positive turn in history,

evidence that our country was leaving behind, or attempting to, a barbarous institution that had blighted the lives of
millions. Such a thing should be celebrated far and wide.

My twinge of possessiveness grew out of the habit of
seeing my home state, and the people who reside there,
as special. The things that happened there couldn't have
happened in other places. Non-Texans could never really
understand what the events that took place in Texas actually meant. I am certain that I'm not alone in this attitude.
From my earliest days, it was drummed into me and, I
believe, other young people growing up in Texas at that
time, that we inhabited a unique place that we were always
supposed to claim, and of which we were always supposed
to be proud. I've noticed over the years, that it is hard to
meet a person from Texas who does not, at some point in
the conversation, let you know, either with a drawl or without, that he or she is from the state.

My proprietary attitude about Juneteenth quickly disappeared. Rather than keeping the holiday to ourselves,
Texans have been in the forefront of trying to make Juneteenth a national holiday. As I think of it, it's really a very
Texas move to say that something that happened in our
state was of enough consequence to the entire nation that
it should be celebrated nationwide. It has been offered, as
part of the justification, that the end of slavery in Texas
was the end of the institution period. That's not quite true.
Granger's order did not end slavery in the country. That did

not happen officially until December 1865, when the Thirteenth Amendment to the Constitution was ratified by the necessary number of states. But it is significant that Texas was the site of the tail end of the Confederate war effort. As the war had been fought to preserve slavery, celebrating Juneteenth throughout the land is a fitting way to mark the end of that effort.

It also is fitting to think of Texas in relation to the nation for another reason. The state has been described as a bellwether for what the United States will become; the term "Texification" has come into use to describe a process that is, supposedly, of recent origin. The history of Juneteenth, which includes the many years before the events in Galveston and afterward, shows that Texas, more than any state in the Union, has always embodied nearly every major aspect of the story of the United States of America. That fact has been obscured by broad caricatures of the state and its people, caricatures that Texans themselves helped to create and helped make the state seem exotic, almost foreign to the rest of the Union.

The essays that follow do not strive to present a chronological narrative of the place where Juneteenth was born. They are, instead, designed to provide a context for an event that has become increasingly important in the life of the American nation. It's a look at history through the medium of personal memoir, a Texan's view of the long road to Juneteenth, the events surrounding the date itself, what happened afterward, and how all of this shaped life in Texas, my family's life, and my own. My Texas roots go deep—on my mother's side back to the 1820s, on my father's side at least to the 1860s. Significantly, my wide-ranging approach to Juneteenth reveals that behind all the broad stereotypes about Texas is a story of Indians, settler colonialists, Hispanic culture in North America, slavery, race, and immigration. It is the American story, told from this most American place.

ON JUNETEENTH

"This, Then, Is Texas"

Texas, perhaps more than any other state in the Union, lives in the public imagination as a place of extremes. How did it get there? Let's start with its size. Until Alaska became a part of the United States in 1959, Texas was the largest state in the Union—268,580 square miles; larger than Kenya, almost three times the size of the United Kingdom. This extended land mass created an early basis for the exaggeration and bragging to which residents of the state are prone. As one observer put it, "exaggeration is often considered to be an endemic low-grade infection of most Texans." Although eclipsed by the nation's vast forty-ninth state, many Texans still cherish their state's distinction as the largest of the lower forty-eight. For them, being the "biggest" in terms of size is unquestionably a good thing, and stands for the state's character, as in "Everything's big in Texas," making the place and the people who live there seem larger than life.

Which part of the state, though, and which people matter most? As for the people, the Cowboy, the Rancher, the Oilman—all wearing either ten-gallon hats or Stetsons—dominate as the embodiments of Texas. Of great importance, as I have said in another context, the image of Texas has a gender and a race: "*Texas is a White man.*" What that means for everyone who lives in Texas and is *not* a White man is part of what I hope to explore in the essays of this book. As for the part of the state that fuels its image, Texas appears in popular culture—movies, songs, television—as part of the West; a setting with cattle kicking up dust in hard dry terrain that when emptied of people gets taken over by tumbleweeds blowing in the wind. While away in college, one of my New England–born and –bred classmates suddenly asked me one day how close I lived to "the desert," and what that was like. I was taken aback. "Very far," I answered. Her question caught me off-guard because I had never seriously thought of my home in relationship to the desert, save for the time I came outside one morning to find my mother's Cutlass Supreme and my father's Ford pickup truck coated with a thin layer of sand from a particularly fierce West Texas dust storm. That may have been the first—and only time—I thought seriously about my connection to the more westerly part of the state.

Livingston, the town where I was born, in more easterly Polk County, and Conroe, the town where I grew up, fifty miles south in Montgomery County, are part of the

Big Thicket; an area covering about 3 million acres in the eastern part of Texas, so named for its dense forests and plant life. The area has been called "North America's Environmental Ark" for ecological "diversity unparalleled in the Earth's Northern Hemisphere." It is estimated that 75 percent of North America's bird species either live in the Big Thicket or spend some time there during their yearly migrations. Montgomery County also reaches into Texas's Gulf Coast Region, putting it, not infrequently, in the path of hurricanes. Very much like its direct neighbor to the south, Harris County, where Houston is located, it has an extremely humid, subtropical climate. In other words, nothing about where I grew up had anything to do with a desert. Like a true Texan, measuring value by size, I suggested to my classmate that the next time she happened to see a topographical map of Texas, she take note of the huge area of green—that could swallow up all of New England— with millions of acres of less forested and more desert-like parts of the state left over. Take that!

There is just so much to misunderstand about Texas, misunderstandings that stem from a general lack of attention to, or even awareness of the state's foundational aspects. Let's start at the most basic level, with the view I suggested to my classmate: topography. The Balcones Escarpment, a raised limestone fault, roughly bisects Texas, separating east from west. The regions on either side have very different ecologies, histories, and, thus, different cultures. A deep irony is that despite the fact that, for most of the state's existence, more people have lived to the east of the Escarpment, it is the inhabitants to the west who have shaped, through cowboy lore and Hollywood films, popular understandings about Texas and the people who live there. West Texas is, stereotypically, the home of two of the figures mentioned above: the Cowboy, riding the range, and the Rancher, owner of the land on which the Cowboy worked. Though both have a history that predates the state's entrance into the American Union in 1845, stretching back into the days when the land was part of New Spain, their images have placed Texas firmly within the American West, with all the tropes, stock characters, and storylines that go with that.

The third figure—the Texas Oilman—of more recent vintage, had his origins in East Texas, but migrated, first to North Texas and then West. The 1956 film *Giant*, based upon Edna Ferber's novel of the same name, explored the cultural conflict that spread across the state in the decades after the legendary oil strike in 1901 at Spindletop established Texas as an oil-producing behemoth. The Oilman soon challenged the Cowboy and the Rancher as the archetypical Texan. Spindletop is about seventy-five miles from where I grew up. Significantly, the film is set, not near Spindletop, which gave rise to Texaco and Gulf Oil companies, or the Humble Oil Field (thirty miles from my hometown), from which Exxon partly descends. Instead, *Giant* was shot in the West Texas town of Marfa, with all

the images of Texas—land and people—blended into one
portrait. The film's opening titles include the jaunty "This,
Then, Is Texas"—the music without the lyrics:

> *Just like a sleeping giant*
> *Sprawling in the sun*
> *In one great hand, the Rio Grande*
> *In the other, Galveston*
>
> *Where oil wells laugh at angels*
> *And buzzards wheel above*
> *This, then, is Texas*
> *Lone Star State of Texas*
> *This, then, is Texas*
> *Land I love*
>
> *Just see the silver dollars*
> *Falling from above*
> *This, then, is Texas*
> *Lone Star State of Texas*
> *This is the giant land I love*
>
> *Austin to Houston*
> *The Alamo, El Paso*
> *Crystal City, Waco*
>
> *Giant, giant, giant, giant . . .*

The film's ranch, Reata, is modeled after the famed million-acre King Ranch, whose mineral leases to the company that would become Exxon helped make the company. I first became familiar with that connection when I worked as a summer law associate at Exxon's headquarters in Houston. Reata is situated on over 800,000 acres of dry and sparsely vegetated land, owned by rancher "Bick" Benedict, played by the lanky Rock Hudson, with an antagonist—the iconic James Dean—as the cowboy-hatted, inarticulate, rope twirling Jett Rink, who would strike oil and become rich overnight. Both men love Leslie Lynnton Benedict, played by the even more iconic Elizabeth Taylor. The conflict between the two White men, wrestling with the natural resources open to people like them—including the prize, Leslie—represent the growing pains of a place that, even today, likes to see itself as a perpetual adolescent on the way to some inevitably bright future.

There is, however, another important figure critically missing from *Giant*, and other defining depictions of Texas, a figure who helped make Juneteenth necessary: the Slave Plantation Owner. Although this species of Texan no longer exists, the influence of the world he (maintaining the gender convention) put in place continues to this day. He resided mainly in what became the populous east, an area developed by the man known as "the Father of Texas," Stephen F. Austin. The Virginia-born and Missouri-raised Austin came to Texas not to create cattle ranches and hire cowboys, but to turn huge swaths of the Mexican province

Coahuila y Tejas into a western version of the cotton fields of Mississippi that had produced such great wealth for plantation owners. What is now the southeastern part of Texas was, in many ways, the perfect place to try this: the soil was amazingly fertile, the growing season long, and there was access to the Gulf of Mexico for shipping harvested crops.

For a number of reasons, including the desire to create defenses against Comanche raids, the Mexican government was eager to have Anglo-Americans come to the area and develop it. There was, however, a problem. Antislavery sentiment was strong in the country only recently separated from Spain. As much as they wanted Whites to come to Texas, most Mexicans were not so keen on them bringing chattel slavery with them. Austin knew that posed a threat to his enterprise. A good number of the Americans who would want to settle on land in this area would hardly want to clear and work that land themselves. They expected to have enslaved people do the clearing and planting, and they would hesitate to move to Texas without assurances that their property rights in enslaved people would be preserved. Austin and his Tejano (ethnic Mexicans living in Texas) partners engaged in intense lobbying to convince Mexican legislators to protect slavery as a way of ensuring the success of their colonization effort. Austin told everyone who would listen that, without slavery, the Anglo colonies would never fully succeed and Americans who came to Texas would surely be poor for the rest of their lives.

Although Austin and his supporters eventually succeeded in gaining exemptions that allowed slavery to continue, the situation remained precarious for them so long
as they were a part of Mexico. The Mexican government
continued to nod toward ending slavery, while the Anglos
and their supporters kept resisting. The matter was settled
when Texans successfully rebelled against Mexico and set
up the Republic of Texas in 1836. With this move, the right
to enslave was secured, and White settlers poured into the
new republic. Texas as its own country lasted but a decade,
all the while beset by poor leadership by some of its presi-
dents, empty coffers after the Panic of 1837, continued conflicts with Mexico, and international pariah status because
it was a slaveholder's republic.

White Texans feared that their new country's
weakness—Mexico remained a potentially formidable
foe—made it vulnerable to calls for abolition, which began
to grow in the 1830s in the United States and among their
trading partners, including Great Britain, which abolished
slavery in 1833. The solution, Anglo-Texans believed, was
to become annexed to the United States. Indeed, that had
been the goal of many Texians (supporters of the break from
Mexico) from the start. This happened in 1845, followed by
the acceptance of Texas as part of the Union. These moves,
controversial because of Texas's status as a slave society, and
President James K. Polk's provocations led to an even more
controversial war with Mexico, which had never accepted

Texas's independence. The United States won the war, and Texas was fully incorporated into the country.

Twenty years after being formally accepted into the American Union, the armed forces of the United States shattered Texas's dream of a cotton-based slave economy when it defeated Texas and its fellow Confederates in the Civil War. Anglo-Texans had been fighting for what they would have called their "way of life" since the 1820s, and had been confident that their alliance with other Southern states would solidify their position. United States Major General Gordon Granger, two years after Abraham Lincoln had issued the Emancipation Proclamation, and two and half months after Lincoln was assassinated, brought the news on June 19, 1865, that the joint effort had not succeeded.

When I was growing up, we took Texas history twice—if I remember correctly, in the fourth and the seventh grades. I cannot say with certainty that slavery was never mentioned. Of course, I didn't need school to tell me that Blacks had been enslaved in Texas. I heard references to slavery from my parents and grandparents. A common retort when another kid—often a sibling—insisted you do something for them you didn't want to do was "Slavery time is over." And we celebrated Juneteenth, which marked the end of the institution. But if slavery was mentioned in the early days of my education, it didn't figure prominently enough in our lessons to give us a clear and complete picture of the role the

institution played in the state's early development, its days
as a Republic, its entry into the Union, and its role in the
Civil War and its aftermath. Instead, as with the claim "The
American Civil War was not about slavery. It was about
states' rights," the move when talking about Texas's rebellion
against Mexico was to take similar refuge in concerns about
overreaching federal authorities. Anglo-Texans chafed at
the centralizing tendencies of the Mexican government
and longed to be free. As one could ask about the states'
rights argument—states' rights to do what?—I don't recall
my teachers giving a complete explanation for why Anglo-
Texans felt so threatened by the Mexican government.

History is, to say the least, complicated. There are almost
always mixed motives within and among individuals about
any of the great issues of the day. Given that two different
ethnic groups, with two different languages, were involved
in Mexican Texas, it's not surprising that cultural tensions
might develop that could lead to a rift, even though the Mexican government had initially welcomed Anglo immigration.
And the Texians were justifiably alarmed by President Santa
Anna's suspension of the Mexican Constitution of 1835 as a
move to consolidate power in the central government. But
contention over slavery had been present from the moment
Stephen Austin, and his father before him, had dreamed
of bringing White colonists to a new version of a promised
land. Many of the people who heeded Austin's call came with
clenched teeth and balled-up fists, so to speak. They arrived

with both insecurity and defiance, knowing that a significant number of people, within Texas and without, viewed their way of life—enslaving people—with abhorrence.

There is no way to get around the fact that, whatever legitimate federalism-based issues were at play, slavery was a central reason Anglo-Texans wanted out of Mexico. Using unpaid labor to clear forests, plant crops, harvest them, and move them to market was the basis of their lives and wealth. As Austin perceptively noted, any individual or family who tried to do this on their own in the wilderness of East Texas would face years of toil and strife without a real prospect of success. Still, nothing is inevitable. Things could have been different. The choice for slavery was deliberate, and that reality is hard to square with a desire to present a pristine and heroic origin story about the settlement of Texas. There is no way to do that without suggesting that the lives of African Americans, and their descendants in Texas, did not, and do not, matter.

It should come as no surprise that my teachers were not inclined to deal with all of this and likely did not know much of this story. They probably were not alone in this regard. As far as my early education went, these aspects of our state history were never fully discussed. When slavery in Texas was mentioned, it was presented as an unfortunate event that was to be acknowledged but quickly passed over. There was no sense of the institution's centrality. Slavery was done. There was no point in dwelling on the past. Texas was all about the future, about what came next—the next cattle drive, the next oil well, the next space flight directed by NASA's Mission Control in Houston.

Except, we *did* dwell on the past. We were exhorted to "Remember the Alamo" and to "Remember Goliad," famous events in Texas's fight for independence from Mexico. Why were those things to be remembered, while the history of an important reason Stephen F. Austin came to Texas, and all that flowed from that fateful decision to put slavery at the heart of Texas, to be forgotten? The question is especially important because while legalized slavery ended, the racially based hierarchy it put in place remained, poisoning the well of social relations in Texas over the ensuing decades. Very significantly, this was not just a matter of a Black/White divide. After the successful creation of Texas, White settlers moved to displace the Tejanos, who had originally welcomed the Anglos as potential allies against Native Americans, people who had their own claims to the land. No other state brings together so many disparate and defining characteristics all in one—a state that shares a border with a foreign nation, a state with a long history of disputes between Europeans and an indigenous population and between Anglo-Europeans and people of Spanish origin, a state that had existed as an independent nation, that had plantation-based slavery and legalized Jim Crow.

Any one of these things would leave a mark on a place. Having them all together almost certainly accounts for Texas's extreme nature, such deep internal complexities creating tensions that roil. All the major currents of American history flow through Texas. As big as it is, that is still a lot for any one state to handle. There is little wonder why the Cowboy would be picked as the most representative figure. Divorced from plantation slavery, coming from a part of the state relatively devoid of Black people, the image of the cowboy on the range quiets the noise a bit and avoids the tragic element in Texas history—the element that Juneteenth supposedly closed the door on, even as it opened another tragic phase in the state and country's history. As painful as it may be, recognizing—though not dwelling on—tragedy and the role it plays in our individual lives, and in the life of a state or nation, is, I think, a sign of maturity.

As the years have gone by, I've had occasion to think more about tragedy and triumph in relationship to Texas, its past, present, and future. It is possible, very likely, actually, that my time there prepared me for the work I do as a historian of the Early American Republic; another moment when triumph and tragedy were inexorably entwined. Disentangling those threads and viewing them critically has been, in fact, a good thing in the context of our national history, broadening our understanding of who we were and who we are now. This same process could do wonders for Texas as well.

Until the middle of the 1960s, Booker T. Washington High School was the virtual center of the Black community in Conroe, Texas, my hometown, with individual churches serving as denominational satellites. It was the school where my mother, Bettye Jean Gordon, taught, her first teaching job after graduating from Atlanta's Spelman College and getting her master's degree at Texas Southern University in Houston. "Booker T.," as it was known, was the "Black school," though at the time it would have been called the "Negro school." It went from kindergarten to twelfth grade. I attended kindergarten at Washington but switched in first grade to Hulon N. Anderson Elementary, a "White school." This act drew a lot of attention to me and my family because that move helped put in motion changes in the racial dynamics of our town.

Around the time I started elementary school, Texas school districts were coming to the end of the road in the decade-long resistance to the 1954 decision *Brown v. Board of Education*. Officials had come up with what they called a "Freedom of Choice" plan as an alternative to mandated desegregation. These plans were adopted all over the South. The expectation was that parents would remain wedded to the schools they knew. White parents would choose "White schools" for their children and Black parents would choose "Black schools" for theirs. The reasons my parents gave for deciding to buck expectations and send me to a "White school" evolved over time as they both became disillusioned with the way integration played out in our town and across the South. The original story, however, was more in line with the civil rights narrative of progress through breaking down legally imposed racial barriers to gain access to better resources. My father, Alfred Gordon, Sr., didn't like K–12 programs, thinking that younger children should be better separated from older kids than the setup at Washington allowed. The White community, as he saw, had elementary schools, intermediate schools, junior high schools, and high schools. The civil rights movement was about opening opportunities to Blacks. The chance to send kids to a school appropriately separated by age, or other issues important to families, was what it was all about. Later, it was simply a matter of my parents having seen the writing on the wall—that courts were eventually going to strike down the freedom-of-choice plans—and deciding to get ahead of the game. It was a matter of pragmatism, not idealistic aspiration.

So, I integrated my town's schools, a la Ruby Bridges, with the chief difference being that I was not escorted to my first day of school by federal marshals. My father drove me and dropped me off. There was a bus route taking White children who lived in the vicinity of my elementary school. But, evidently, it was decided that it would be best that I not take it. I learned later that my parents and the school district negotiated about how it would all proceed. No fuss would be made. My parents would not talk to the press about it. I would just arrive at school and begin first grade as if there were nothing to it. There was, of course something to it. This was a new thing in our little corner of East Texas. There were threats against my family—which I also didn't learn of until later—but nothing came of them.

William Faulkner famously wrote, in his 1951 novel *Requiem for a Nun*, "the past is never dead. It's not even past." I believe the Nobel laureate was wrong about that. The past is dead. But, like other formerly living things, echoes of the past remain, leaving their traces in the people and events of the present and future. A bit of history, then, is needed for context. East Texas had been the locus of slavery and the plantation system even before Texas became a state. The legacy of that time, and its baked-in racial hierarchy, survived long after enslaved people were freed. Texans who had enslaved Blacks and been defeated in the Civil War turned on the freed people with a vengeance, seeking to maintain the control they had during slavery. Along with

Jim Crow, one of the chief means of doing this was extra-legal violence. Private citizens, along with law enforcement, either directly or by looking the other way, often resorted to this mechanism of control.

Montgomery County, of which Conroe was the county seat during my childhood, was known for being particularly harsh for Black people. Just to mention the more publicized examples, in 1885, twenty years after the end of the Civil War, in the town of Montgomery, just seven miles from Conroe, Bennett Jackson, a young Black man, was lynched after being charged with breaking into a home and assaulting a White woman and her children. That Jackson would be lynched was well known ahead of time, as it turned into a public celebration for White citizens in the area. Men, women, and children gathered and had a picnic to watch. The *Houston Post* reported on the spectacle, explaining that White residents wanted to send a message to Black people who were considered to be acting in too forward a manner.

The message went not only to Blacks, but to Whites, telling them what they could do to Blacks without fear. This knowledge operated along a continuum, from lynching down to nonlethal displays of disrespect without consequence. After the events in nearby Montgomery, Conroe was the site of other notorious incidents that raised the town's profile on the question of race. In 1922, a Black man, Joe Winters, was burned alive at the stake on the courthouse square after a teenaged girl accused him of rape.

And in 1940 there was the case of *Texas v. White*, which garnered much attention and was the subject of a Supreme Court opinion.

Bob White had come to Livingston, Texas, the town where I was born, at the request of his mother, who wanted him to help her pick cotton on a place that was still called a plantation. In 1936, he was accused of raping Ruby Cochran, a White woman in town. The authorities brought about fifteen Black men who were working in the cotton field to have Cochran identify the man who raped her. She could not identify her attacker by sight, but she ultimately identified White by his voice, after the authorities had him speak words she had evidently told them the assailant had said during the assault. After being arrested and put in jail, the Texas Rangers took White into the woods nightly for a week, chained him to a tree, beat him severely, and threatened to kill him if he did not confess. They prepared a statement for him to sign, though he could neither read nor write. During this initial period, he had no lawyer and was not allowed to speak with anyone. He was found guilty in the first trial and sentenced to die in the electric chair. The case was appealed, and a new trial was ordered. This time the trial was removed to Conroe because the atmosphere in Livingston was too charged. White was convicted again.

The case went all the way up to the Supreme Court of the United States. Writing for the Court in 1941, Justice Hugo Black held that the confession, obtained by severe beatings and keeping White incommunicado, violated the Due Process Clause of the Fourteenth Amendment. With that, the case went back down for retrial. It was during the final proceeding in Conroe, in June of 1941, that W. S. "Dude" Cochran, Ruby Cochran's husband, walked to the front of the courtroom and shot White in the back of the head, killing him instantly. He handed the gun to the prosecutor and turned himself over to the sheriff. He was arrested and was out on a bond of $500. His trial, held a few days later, lasted three hours. After the prosecutor's closing statement, the courtroom erupted in applause and cheers. The jury deliberated for two minutes and returned a verdict of "not guilty," and Cochran walked out of court a free man after having murdered Bob White in an open courtroom in front of the judge, lawyers, and dozens of spectators.

These events tore at the heart of the Black community in Conroe and Livingston. As accustomed as they were to the atmosphere created by small-town White supremacy, these deep transgressions drove home their situation. The lynching of Joe Winters was pure terrorism, of course; a gruesome spectacle of murder-to-send-a-message. With White, I think of the hopes that must have been raised by all the procedural moves that landed the case in the Supreme Court of the United States, which found a violation of the Constitution, only to have those hopes dashed when a man and his community decided to take the law into their own hands. It was not Cochran alone who ignored the rule of law. The judge, lawyers, law enforcement, and White townspeople did so as well, just as surely as the Texas Rangers did when they illegally tortured Bob White.

The Winters and White stories had something in common, besides the cliché of hysteria surrounding the taboo of Black men and White women. In both situations, Blacks offered an alternative version of what had happened. They insisted that the teenaged girl had been caught in the woods with Winters, having gone there voluntarily. Embarrassment about being found with a Black man led to the charge of rape. As for the White case, my stepgrandfather, who knew Bob White and the Cochrans, insisted that Bob White and Ruby Cochran had been "going together." White, apparently, talked freely about it. When her husband discovered the liaison, things proceeded from there. After White's murder, and no doubt knowing about Winters, one of my great-great-aunts, who had helped raise my mother, vowed to never spend the night in Conroe again.

What to make of these counter narratives, of course, is central to writing history. For many years, Blacks like the ones in Conroe and Livingston—all over the country, really—have had their stories written out of history. The tyranny of ideas about "the archive," or what constitutes the official record, all too often, has buried their knowledge and rendered it suspect. This is so despite the fact that it is well known that such people were operating under an oppression that deliberately prevented them from creating parts of the archive or making official records. What is the morality that would say that the oppressors' version of historical events should naturally take precedence over the knowledge of the oppressed? How could any judgment created by the people who watched Dude Cochran shoot Bob White in the back of the head and let him walk away with no consequences, or who planned and gathered at a picnic to watch a man be murdered, be presented as neutral and credible?

Some years ago, a reporter, doing a story about a rape allegation, interviewed me about the phenomenon described in the Winters and White cases—White women saying (or people saying it for them) they had been raped after their liaisons with Black men came to light. As we talked, it became clear that he desperately wanted me to refute the idea that this ever happened. I had never, until that time, spoken with a reporter doing a news story who seemed so invested in a particular idea. I could hear him become more and more frustrated as I pushed back against his obvious certainty that these stories were all lies. The reporter had no idea how strong the taboo against interracial sex between Black men and White women has been, no understanding that a White woman found to have welcomed the advancements of a Black man would likely be banished from her family and White society, if not subjected to violence.

In any event, it would take a long time to escape a history like the one made in Conroe, if escape were even possible.

It would certainly take longer than the nearly twenty-five years separating White's murder-without-consequence from my entering Anderson Elementary to erase the culture created during postslavery Texas. My first-grade teacher, Mrs. Daughtry, however, could not have handled my time in her care any better. Indeed, the principal, Mr. Moorhead, and every teacher with whom I came into contact seemed committed to rising above the town's history to make things work. I never experienced any different treatment from them. In fact, I felt nothing but their support.

There was the oddity of being on display. Periodically, small groups of visitors–educators, I assume—would show up and stand in the doorway of the classroom to observe how things were going, a Black child in a room with maybe twenty-five other White students. Not to take anything away from the teachers and administrators at Anderson, but I did make things easy for them. First, and perhaps most important of all, there was, for a time, only me. One Black child was not exactly an invasion. The degree of racial tolerance among Whites has always been about numbers. Also, I was a good student right off the bat. In those days, when people cared less about making children feel bad, I was a "Bluebird"—the group for the best readers. There was no attempt to hide what was going on from the slower-reading "birds." We got letter grades in our subjects, and the local newspaper printed the names of kids who were on the "Honor Roll," and my name appeared there.

My great-great-aunt—the one who would not stay overnight in Conroe, who lived in Houston and was also quite
extravagant—bought boxes and boxes of dresses, tights,
blouses, skirts, and hats from the most upscale department
store in the city at the time, Sakowitz. I remember opening
them with my mother and being overwhelmed at the number and range of choices. I could go a long time without
repeating an outfit. What it must have meant for my aunt,
born on a farm into the even more racially repressive and
violent society Texas was at the end of the nineteenth century, to be present at this moment when one of her young
relatives was about to embark upon an adventure in this
brave new world. Making sure I was dressed to the nines
was her contribution to the civil rights movement.

This period was intense—my mother remembers me
breaking out in hives at one point, a thing I don't recall.
Perhaps some of those initial hard memories were lost
among all the things that happened next. Over my four
years at Anderson, I enjoyed school and looked forward to
going. I made friends, almost always boys, who were more
steadfast in their friendships than the girls I encountered—
David, Richard, Alan, Lee, Dennis, John, Brett, but only
Sharla, Pam, and Vicky. I was far too sensitive for "One day
I like you. The next day I don't like you," which is what I
more often encountered in the world of girls at my school.
As my parents predicted, in 1968, the Supreme Court, in
Green v. County School Board of New Kent County, Virginia,

struck down the freedom-of-choice plans as the subter-fuges to avoid *Brown* that they were. With that, the process of integrating all the schools in Conroe began in earnest for other kids, including my older brothers.

All of this certainly made me focus more consciously on the racial landscape in my town and in Texas. I had been aware of it, to some degree, before my adventures at Anderson began. It could not have been avoided. When I went to Sadler Clinic, where our family doctor practiced, I knew there were two separate entrances, one leading into the waiting room for Blacks and the other, into the wait-ing room for Whites. The receptionist sat in a room with windows facing out into either waiting room so that she could handle patients based on race. As we checked in, or settled the bill, I could see into the other area, and noted how much larger and better appointed it was, with a bigger variety of magazines. Even at that young age, the magazine deficit bothered me the most. That Whites would be given more to read really upset me more than the fact that our waiting room was so small that we sometimes spilled onto the sidewalk leading up to the clinic. When we went to the movies at the old-styled Crighton Theater, Blacks had to sit in the balcony. This went on, as I think of it, even after the *de jure* segregation had ceased. But the power of habit, bol-stered by a silent undercurrent of intimidation and fear, was strong. The faint echoes of Bennett, Winters, and White reverberated.

I knew what was happening with me, and with other Black children, was a matter of law, which I understood broadly as the rules of what could be done in society and what could not be done. I also knew that law wasn't the only thing. The law might say I could go to a school or into a store. But it could not ensure that I would be welcome when I came to these places. I had vivid examples of this all around. There was a store near the border between our neighborhood and a White neighborhood whose proprietor was extremely hostile to the Black people who came into his store. We—my brothers and I—were told not to go there and spend our nickels and dimes to buy cookies or bubblegum, and to be talked to roughly by an angry old White man. Of course, I didn't always live by that rule. Sometimes while riding my banana seat bike, I would duck into the place—its hardwood floors and carefully arranged products appealed to me—to get some item, or I would be with friends and their parents who didn't boycott the store. I remember the forbidding atmosphere, his cold glare as I paid for whatever treat I had come to buy. It was puzzling. I knew I had done nothing to provoke this strong reaction. Perhaps my experiences are the reason I have no nostalgia for the old-style small-town general store, where customers were supposedly treated better than in large, so-called impersonal places like Walmart. Not all of them, but many White storeowners in these little towns were gratuitously mean to us.

I felt the same puzzlement at my classmates, some of whom were quite hostile, while others seemed friendly but then surprised me at crucial moments when strong racial animus would appear seemingly out of the blue. Each morning the milk truck would come by our classes, and we were given a carton of milk. My mother didn't want me drinking chocolate milk every day. So, the crate for our class would arrive with one lone red and white half-pint carton amid the group of brown and white ones. I was the only person in my class who got the carton of white milk. One day, after some argument with a girl who was normally friendly, I was surprised to hear her, all of seven years old, shout at me, "That's why you always drink white milk. Because you want to be White, like us!" Her outburst stopped me in my tracks, the idiocy of it immediately striking me almost as funny. How ridiculous was the idea that drinking milk would make me White—that I would think that? How ridiculous to think that I *wanted* to be White!

This was one of many lessons I learned. I had considered this girl a friend, but her outburst revealed that despite our friendly connection, the bottom line was, there is "us" and there is "you." I learned a similar lesson when I would see my school friends in town with their parents and siblings, say, at a local store and my greeting to them would be met with total silence. They knew, at that young age, that their friendliness toward me might draw rebukes from their relatives. But then there was the family of girls at Anderson who always asked me to play with them even though they were not in my class. They were very poor, I could tell. Someone, their mother likely, had made clothes for them out of the same material. I sensed, by their manner, that they were sincere. They taught me that not all White people are the same.

For the most part, however, I took it as a given that Black people and White people were, for reasons I didn't understand, at odds with one another. Or more precisely, I had the impression that the root of the problem was that "they" meaning Whites, didn't like us, and that is why we didn't get along—in much the same way one might say "dogs don't like cats, and that's why they don't get along." When we see a particular dog and cat getting along—like me and the girls wearing homemade dresses from the same material—we can chalk that up to the truth that there are exceptions to every rule. The general rule stands, nevertheless. One thing I *never* thought, however, was that there was anything wrong with me, something for which I will always be grateful to my parents. I knew I had not done anything to the store owner or the kids who were unkind to me. It was very clear in my mind that this was a problem of their own making. The real puzzling thing for me was why they were making the problem.

Looking back—and I would not have thought of this then—it is very likely that what was going on in the world outside of our town made the angry store owner, and the many others like him, even angrier. Black people in the United States, even ones in our area, were demanding changes to the way things were done in society. Their challenges were meeting with success nationally with the passage of legislation and court decisions that dismantled *de jure* segregation. It must have appeared that the floodgates were opening, and all the old verities that had held southern society in place would be swept away. This was far from the truth, but they must have felt the balance of power was shifting in society. And this was the sixties. Even young Whites were protesting the war in Vietnam, a particularly sore point among Whites in my area, and creating something called a "counterculture." A White man of this sort, in particular—not a southern grandee, but a storeowner who worked in his own store—had much to lose. Empowered Black people made the intangible benefits derived from Whiteness less valuable.

It was never just about money, or else the angry store owner would have welcomed the Black dollars that could enrich him further. Being a White man, entitled to deference, with the right to vote, and hold office—entitled to hold on to power—to be the kind of person who could walk into a courtroom, shoot a Black man in front of dozens of spectators, and get away with it, placed him above Black people, whether he had money or not. Most important of all, it placed him above Black men. Patriarchy, which is not only about the subjugation of women but about competition between males, is so central to this story. White males had, since the days of slavery, arrogated to themselves the right to have access to all types of women in society, while strictly prohibiting Black males access to White women, on many occasions becoming murderous about that stricture. The crowds who picnicked while Bennett Jackson was killed, who gathered to watch Joe Winters be burned at the stake, who acquiesced in the murder of Bob White, were participating in affirmations, and celebrations, of their power. Not that they would have wanted to be there, but Blacks were excluded from these spectacles. Before Winters was killed, law enforcement blocked roads leading into Conroe, telling Black people who approached that they could not come to town, explaining to them what was about to happen.

As for my own situation, matters were more complicated than just Whites' reaction to my leaving Washington for Anderson. Some members of the Black community felt that my parents were making a statement—alas, a negative one—about the quality of teaching and education at Washington. That my mother taught there made things even more complicated. Was she suggesting, by her actions, that she and her colleagues were not capable? *Brown* had proceeded under the declaration that separate schools were inherently unequal, part of a legal strategy that at least some of the parents in the *Brown* litigation rejected. In towns all over the South, the schools in Black communities were a source of pride that inspired loyalty.

Except for my father's later-in-life explanation for what had happened—that he didn't like Washington's kindergarten through twelfth-grade program—there was no indication that my parents thought there was anything wrong with the school. It was not a comment on the teachers. That they kept my two brothers there suggests it really was a matter of my being at the beginning of things, less wedded to Washington than my brothers, who had been there for years in elementary school. And, despite their later disillusionment, my parents had, in fact, been idealistic. Still, I became something of a controversial figure at age six. For years after that, people I didn't know, knew me; and that knowledge either made them inclined to be very positive toward me, or to be very negative.

I remember standing in line, one bright sunny day, waiting for the bus, soon after the process of desegregation had taken hold. Kids from the adjacent school, Crockett (yes, named for Davy) would come over to catch the bus at Anderson. I heard an older boy, who was Black, say to his companions who were also Black, "That's her!" I was in the adjoining line, perhaps two people behind him. He turned around in his line, reached over the people standing between us, and began to punch me repeatedly in the chest, as hard as he could. I was shocked and terrified. I had no idea who this person was, or why he was hitting me. His expression held such hatred.

Memory is funny. When I call this episode to mind,

I don't feel the actual physical pain I know I felt that day. What I remember is really just a version of what it felt like to have his fist pounding into my chest. Despite the reality of that, the moment was also surreal, breaking the rules of cause and effect. Having done nothing to this boy, his attack was outlandish. I had a hunch that going to adults about this would likely make things worse. For some children, bringing adults into the picture just fuels the fire. I never told my parents. Older brothers come in handy in situations like this. I told my brothers what had happened. One confronted the boy, evidently did a little pounding himself, and the boy never bothered me again.

As the years passed, there were other, less intense, moments like that. People I didn't know wanted to fight me or threatened to beat me up. If a cartoonist were to draw pictures of these encounters, the expression on my face would be a combination of fear and utter confusion. The thought bubble would say, *"Who are you?"* I understand now in a way that I did not then, that the "you" in that question was a person who felt a sense of deep loss. I was seen, wrongly, as the catalyst for that loss. The courts, not I, had mandated desegregation. If that had not happened, I would have continued on by myself at Anderson, and gone on to whatever feeder school came afterward. The details of how all of this had come about didn't filter down to the kids who challenged me. I was a symbol of their loss.

What was that loss? The move toward integration

may have killed off one bad thing—Jim Crow education, which would never have truly provided equal funding for two, separate educational systems in the town—but it took some valuable things with it. The notion of "separate" being *inherently* unequal didn't take account of what it meant for Black students to have Black teachers, particularly at that precise moment in history. Strong bonds existed between teachers and students at Booker T. They were neighbors, relatives (in some cases), and fellow church members. The bonds forged in the classrooms were solidified outside the school, suffusing every aspect of the lives of students and teachers. The "classroom" was everywhere, really.

I had no doubt that my teachers at Anderson cared about me. But, it was different. Outside of school, we had no real point of connection. There is no way that Mrs. Daughtry, or Mrs. Gilliland, my second-grade teacher, as lovely as they were to me, could know me as well as the teachers at Washington knew their students. My teachers and I shared a common culture as Texans, but that culture had been subdivided by race. And, again, I was a model student. What would it be like for children who were not as prepared for school as I had been by my mother; kids who were not as even-tempered and didn't have a fancy wardrobe?

Sometimes, while playing with friends in my neighborhood after school, the jump rope would drop and kids would disappear into their homes. I soon learned the reason for the drill: They had spotted their teacher's car coming down the road. They didn't want her—it was usually Mrs. Dancy—to see them outside playing when they should be inside studying and doing their homework. I don't think I would have had a response like that if I had seen one of my teachers riding through the neighborhood. I wouldn't have thought that they had any claim on my time away from school; or that I had to impress them by my willingness to give up play time. Clearly, there was something extra going on here.

I can't say it was the case with all Black teachers of my mother's generation, who had come of age in the South, as she did, but I know from her life and from the way her colleagues responded to me, that many of them saw themselves as on a mission. Education was about the individual students, just as it was for my teachers at Anderson, but there was an additional component; an explicit mission of race uplift. My teachers at Anderson did not have to concern themselves with that. Except for the few Black students in their classes, their students were not the descendants of people who had been specifically denied the chance to be educated, and then having their enslavement, or second-class status, justified by, among other things, their lack of education. Becoming educated was an act of resistance. The classroom was a site of that resistance. Along with ministers, many of whom also saw racial uplift as part of their task, schoolteachers were among the most respected members of the Black community. These women and men were role models, charged with preparing the next generation of Black children to take the steps toward community advancement. I remember vividly once, when I was in intermediate school, showing my report card to Mrs. Reece, my mother's best friend, who was the librarian at Washington. Expecting praise, I noticed the slight frown on her face. She zeroed in on the two B's on my report. "When people are given the ability to do better. They should do better," she said.

The effects of integration on schoolchildren, Black and White, has received a great amount of attention over the years. What has been much less considered is the effect that integration had on the Black teachers who were in Black schools when the changes initially came. Many of them, including in my town, were taken out of the classroom. The children were to be integrated, not the teaching staff. Putting Black teachers at the head of classrooms of mainly White students was never the school district's priority. People who had been figures of authority were put in charge of dispensing books and doing other administrative tasks that took them away from contact with Black students, depriving those students of daily role models.

My mother was not taken out of the classroom. She was one of a group of Black teachers chosen to go to White schools, and she moved to Conroe High School to teach tenth-grade English. Not to idealize the days of segregation too much, but with that move, she lost the daily companionship of a full cadre of Black teachers, mainly female, with whom she had much in common. It would be many years before she found true equilibrium with her new colleagues, none of whom were used to dealing with Black people as equals. She maintained friendly relations with them, gaining some true friends. She was respected, and was actually relied on for her extraordinary abilities—she was a whiz at creating lesson plans, and did so for many years. But there were occasional slights and cultural mishaps as the White teachers at Conroe High, whose closest contacts with Blacks were likely their maids or the nanny who raised them, tried to figure out how to deal with my mother. She always loved being in the classroom, and understood the importance of the choice she and my father had made about my education. But she, too, also felt a profound sense of loss.

My mother confessed, later in life, that while she took joy in all of her students, she had become a teacher "to teach Black students." "I can't talk to them the way we used to," she'd say. What she meant was that it was harder to address Black students in the classroom, and talk openly about their common mission of moving the Black community ahead; reminding them that this was a large part of what their education was about. That message had no place in what were now her predominately White classes. The mission of a lifetime had to evolve.

Integration also changed Black students over time. A good number of them soon discounted the notion that they were any different than their White counterparts. After all, Blacks and Whites were in school together. The new Sadler Clinic, much expanded and modernized, was fully integrated. People, Black and White, could sit wherever they wanted in the North Hills Cinema—the successor to the Crighton—which was in the town's first shopping center. By all outward appearances things were "equal." What mission did they have? The mask often slipped to reveal that things had not changed as much as some may have thought, and that integration was more about Blacks coming to Whites rather than a mutual engagement. Perhaps a small but telling thing: Booker T. Washington became the integrated "Washington Intermediate School." I returned there for fifth and sixth grade, going back to where I had been in kindergarten. But the name was now simply "Washington," with no designation of whether it was "George" or "Booker T." Integration meant that Blacks came under the jurisdiction of White teachers and schools. White children, overwhelmingly, kept White teachers, and did not go to schools explicitly named for Black people.

And there were life-and-death issues, too. In 1973, an eighteen-year-old Black male, Gregory Steele, a classmate of one of my brothers, was arrested and taken to jail for fighting. He never made it out. He was shot twice and killed. According to the official story, Steele pulled a knife

or razor on the police officers, even though he had supposedly been searched while at the police station. I remember
Steele as a lanky, quiet young man with close-cropped hair
in that era of Afros. Christmas that year, two days after
Steele was killed, was a more somber affair in our community. Our hearts were too heavy for unbridled celebration.
As in the earlier cases, the Black community had a different
story about Steele. I heard that, to the consternation of her
parents, Steele had been secretly dating a White girl. Her
father was said to have been a friend of Darwin Bryant, the
officer who shot Steele. Steele had been warned to leave her
alone. In some ways, the Steele case could be cited as evidence of at least some measure of progress. Officer Bryant
was actually charged and brought to trial, though he was
eventually acquitted.

My hometown is nearly unrecognizable today. Now
listed as the fastest-growing city in the country, the place
that had fewer than 5,000 inhabitants when my family
moved there when I was an infant now boasts a population of over 87,000. What had been a pine forest between
Conroe and Houston is now nearly all filled in. The area
is slated to get ever bigger as Exxon, which grew out of
the old Humble Oil Field, has moved its headquarters
back home, bringing a massive number of people with it.
The changes had started even before I went off to college
in New England. In the summer between college and law
school, I worked in a government office in the Montgomery

County Courthouse, on the same site where Joe Winters had been burned alive, fifty-nine years before. There have now been, and are, Black principals of schools—something that would have been unthinkable in my childhood. The schools are integrated, with a new group that was not present during my childhood. There were virtually no Hispanic children in the schools I attended as a child, the town being made up largely of Whites of English and German origin and Black people. That situation has changed markedly as Hispanic, and now Asian, students have become more of a presence in what now must be called a city. In downtown Conroe, on a wall that used to have an old advertisment for soda that I thought clever, is a mural of me and, in a nearby park, a bust. It would be almost impossible to convey to children who live there now how different their Conroe is from the one I knew.

CHAPTER

3

Origin Stories: Africans in Texas

It's a safe bet that most people in the United States, when they think of it, believe that Black people first appeared in North America in 1619. The story of the "20. and odd negroes" that John Rolfe announced, in matter of fact fashion, to have arrived in Virginia that year is often taken as the beginning of what we might call "Black America"—from that twenty, to 4 million—by the time of Emancipation in 1865—to nearly 40 million today. Historians study those earliest years to, among other things, pinpoint the beginning of American slavery (what was the status of those first 20?) and to find early traces of cultural memories from Africa. They also look to this time to see if they can discover how deeply ideas about race were embedded in the culture of the people who had established the English colony in Virginia. The Africans, of different ethnic groups, and a heterogeneity of backgrounds seldom acknowledged, certainly had ideas about the English, but were so few in number, and so far outside of power, that they could not impose their will through law on their captors, nor were any of their thoughts recorded.

Origin stories matter, for individuals, groups of people, and for nations. They inform our sense of self; telling us what kind of people we believe we are, what kind of nation we believe we live in. They usually carry, at least, a hope that where we started might hold the key to where we are in the present. We can say, then, that much of the concern with origin stories is about our current needs and desires (usually to feel good about ourselves), not actual history. History is about people and events in a particular setting and context, and how those things have changed over time in ways that make the past different from our own time, with an understanding that those changes were not inevitable. Origin stories often seek to find the familiar, or the superficially familiar—memory, sometimes shading into mythology. Both memory and mythology have their uses, even if they must be separated from our understandings about the demands of historical thinking.

Consider the difference between the stories of Plymouth, Massachusetts, and those of Jamestown, Virginia. Plymouth Rock gives Americans a founding story about a valiant people leaving their homes to escape religious persecution, and founding a new society in the wilderness, with the aid of friendly Indigenous people, like Squanto (Tisquantum) of the Patuxet. Who among those who grew up in the United States did not perform in, or watch, school plays telling the story of these encounters, or make cutouts of turkeys symbolizing the first Thanksgiving feast that the Pilgrims and Patuxets shared—in most cases, I would wager, without knowing the name of the Indian group involved or Squanto's true name? In recent years the story of "the Pilgrims and the Indians" has fallen out of favor in many quarters, as people have come to think more realistically about the interactions between the English settlers and groups like the Patuxet. Despite that reassessment, two centuries of telling the Pilgrims' story in the traditional way continues to shape attitudes about the beginnings of what would become our country.

At the other end of the scale, we have the narrative of Jamestown, created more openly as an economic venture in 1607. It is difficult to wrest an uplifting story from the doings of English settlers who created the colony for no purpose other than making money or, at least, to make a living for themselves. Not long after their arrival, they started down a path that would make Virginia a full-fledged slave society, the largest and richest of the thirteen colonies. What little I learned about Jamestown as a child centered on the story of Pocahontas (Matoaka), the daughter of Powhatan, who serves the same function as Squanto in the Pilgrim story, to emphasize the triumph of amity over enmity between the Indigenous people and the English settlers, something very different than what actually happened.

Pocahontas lives in legend and song as having "had a very mad affair" with Captain John Smith, a leader in Jamestown, a tale prompted by his memoirs that speak of her having risked her life to keep her father from killing him. The more salient—historical—point is that she married and had a son with John Rolfe, a union that did settle, for a time, the relations between her people and the English. I am certain nearly every American schoolchild of my generation learned of Pocahontas, though one of my college classmates assured me that her elementary school in New England had downplayed the Virginia settlement and focused mainly on the Pilgrims as the beginning of America as we know it. Jamestown was mentioned, she said, but as a brief experiment of little lasting consequence. *"We learned there were some people down there,"* she said with a wave of her hand. I imagine that is how most Americans in the past were taught to view the two colonies. As famous as the Pocahontas–John Smith narrative may be, the story of America is often portrayed as having started in Pilgrim/ Puritan–influenced New England.

There is also a version of this attitude about Plymouth versus Jamestown in the origin story of African Americans. I remember hearing in school, probably because I was in Texas, stray references to a man of African descent—a "Negro"—named Esteban (Estebanico), who was in what would become Texas during the time of Spanish exploration. Interestingly enough, he arrived in the area of the future Galveston, where General Granger would proclaim the end of slavery in Texas over three hundred years later. The last phrase, "during the time of Spanish exploration," signaled that this was information about a world gone by that we didn't have to pay much attention to, as it had little to do with understandings about the history of our country. Estebanico, who was wandering (actually) around Texas—eventually across Texas—in the 1520s with the famous Álvar Núñez Cabeza de Vaca, appeared as a singular figure. I hadn't been told that other people of African descent—some enslaved, some not—arrived with the Spanish when they came to the Americas. Whether enslaved or free, these people were disconnected from the institution of plantation slavery that developed in Texas three centuries later, the institution that helped define my ancestors' circumstances.

The same phenomenon applies to St. Augustine, Florida, which was not at all a part of my early education. It was there, in fact, that racially based slavery, as an organized system, began on American soil, established by the Spanish as early as 1565. The story of Africans in St. Augustine is rich, as there is documentation of their presence and lives in surviving parish records and historical accounts of the conflicts that arose between enslaved people and their Spanish captors and between the Spanish and the English who fought over the territory for decades. In 1735 the Spanish governor chartered a settlement for enslaved Africans who escaped from the English colonies and made it to

St. Augustine. The only condition for protection was that the new residents adopt Catholicism and swear allegiance to the Spanish king. The settlement of free Blacks existed until the Spanish sold Florida to the United States in 1817.

I had heard of St. Augustine by the time I got to college. But it, too, was in the category *"there were some people down there."* The English had "won" the contest against the Spanish in North America—in Texas and in Florida. What was the point of incorporating this story of Africans and Spanish people into the general narrative of American history or, more specifically, the history of African Americans? The same could be said of the French, in their beaver-trapping colonies near the Great Lakes. They were "also-rans" in the race for the territory that became the United States. The French influence in Louisiana—its civil law approach to marriage (which it shares with Texas), the French Quarter in New Orleans, Cajuns (descendants of the people exiled in the eighteenth century from the French Colony Acadia by the victorious British)—has been treated as mere seasoning for a culture almost universally recognized as Anglo-American. The brief period of Dutch slave ownership in New York is almost totally out of the picture.

All of this was the result of a nationalist-oriented history, with an intense focus on what was going on within the boundaries of the United States, and seeing what was going on almost totally from the perspective of English-speaking (and White) people. The world enclosed in that way left out so much about the true nature of life in Early America, about all the varied influences that shaped the people and circumstances during those times. It closes off the vital understanding about contingency, how things could have taken a different turn. Very significantly, it helped create and maintain an extremely narrow construction of Blackness.

Under the conventional narrative with which most Americans, it is safe to say, are familiar, Blacks came to North America under the power of the English from places that were never clearly defined, for where they came from didn't matter much. They went from speaking the languages of their homelands to speaking English. They worked on plantations in the fields or in the house. This highly edited origin story winds the Black experience tight, limiting the imaginative possibilities of Blackness—what could be done by people in that skin. To be sure, the institution of slavery itself circumscribed the actions of enslaved African Americans, but it never destroyed their personhood. They did not become a separate species by the experience of being enslaved. All of the feelings, talents, failings, strengths and weaknesses—all the states and qualities that exist in human beings—remained in them. There has been too great a tendency within some presentations of enslaved people to lose sight of that fact, in ways obvious and not.

For example, we can see it in the treatment of that most basic of human traits: the ability to acquire and to speak a language. Language, however formed, connects

people to one another. Dutch was the first language of
noted abolitionist Sojourner Truth, born Isabella Baum-
free in Swartekill, New York, near the end of the 1790s.
She almost certainly spoke English with a Dutch-inflected
accent. Yet, reproductions of her speech were written in
the stereotypical dialect universally chosen to portray the
speech of enslaved Blacks, no matter where in the country they lived. Under this formulation, the experiences
of growing up hearing and speaking Dutch had no effect
upon Truth. It was as if the legal status of being enslaved,
and the biological reality of having been born of African
descent, fixed her pattern of speech, almost as a matter of
brain function.

When I was working on my first book, writing about
the way historians had handled the story of Thomas Jefferson and Sally Hemings, I noticed that one line of attack
on the veracity of Madison Hemings, who said in recollections that he was the son of Jefferson and Hemings, was to
suggest that the statements he gave to the journalist Sam-
uel Wetmore were unreliable because it was unlikely that
a former enslaved person could speak in standard English.
The notion that such a thing could happen was treated as
presumptively incredible. Even a brief thought about the
circumstances of Hemings's life, viewing him as a human
being, however, would tell a different story about his narrative. Hemings's recollections make clear that his older
siblings—Beverley (a male) and Harriet—left Monticello

to live as White people. Both married White people who may not have known that their spouses were partly Black and had been born enslaved. The communities they lived in, Washington, D.C., and Maryland, evidently, did not know that either. Many years after the pair left Monticello, their younger brother, Eston, would follow his older siblings into the White world, settling his family in Madison, Wisconsin.

How did Madison Hemings's siblings live convincingly as White if they spoke in the dialect universally applied to enslaved people? Why would Madison—the middle son between the older Beverley and Harriet and the younger, Eston—speak differently than his siblings? Realizing that the actual circumstances of the Hemings children's lives mattered, and should have been taken into account, would have made clear that it made no sense to assume that Hemings could not have spoken in the way portrayed in his conversation with Wetmore.

A similar analysis, or lack of analysis, has often been at play in writing about the Hemings children's mother, Sally. As I have traveled the country talking about the books I have written about the Hemings family, I've been struck by the responses to the fact that Sally Hemings, and her brother James, learned to speak French during their years in France. On several occasions I have been asked, with seeming wonder, "how" they could have learned to speak French. And even when the question is not specifically raised, it seems to hang in the air when people ponder the fact that she, and presumably her brother, thought for a time to remain in Paris when Jefferson decided to go home. *How could they have gotten along there? They didn't speak the language.* Doubts about their basic capacities persist, despite the differences in their circumstances and opportunities in France. Both siblings had been working for wages. James, formally trained as a chef and acting as chef de cuisine at Jefferson's residence, the Hôtel de Langeac, supervised French servants. Because slavery in the United States was racially based, it was easy to graft the legally imposed incapacities of slavery onto Black people as a group, making incapacity an inherent feature of the race.

Perhaps there is something about French, for a long time the language of diplomacy and culture. It is considered "fancy" in a way that goes along with the country's cuisine and vaunted high fashion—haute cuisine, haute couture. What of individuals born at the lowest rung of society? Could enslaved people, Black people, ever lay claim to sophistication? Over one hundred years after James Hemings's and Sally Hemings's time in France, Secretary of State William Jennings Bryan, while contemplating a crisis in Haiti, exclaimed, "Dear me. Think of it. N*****s speaking French."

It is hard to imagine that Bryan seriously thought that learning a language, which human beings do quite well without formal instruction—uneducated babies do it all the time—was really beyond the ken of Black people. He cannot have been that ignorant. Instead, he was more likely following a well-worn path: the "joke" that sends a vicious message through supposedly lighthearted humor. So much of racism is about announcing, in various ways, the agreed-upon fictions about Black people that justify attempting to keep them in a subordinate status; like the inanity that children produced from the union of a Black person and a White person were sterile, like a mule, in either the first or a later generation. William Faulkner, who almost certainly knew better, repeated this obviously false notion, it has been suggested, for shock value. Or, perhaps, he was drunk during these moments.

The fiction that has African Americans naturally speaking in a particular way, or unable to learn a language, slyly promotes the notion that Blacks are somewhat less than human, in their inability to master a human trait: the capacity to engage in complex communication. At the very least, the ideas about Blacks and language serve as means to convey the supposed gulf that exists between the races. Administrators involved in the WPA Slave Narrative Project of the 1930s, which gathered the recollections of formerly enslaved people, engaged in a concerted effort to render the speech of the interviewees into stereotypical Black dialect. As a result, the accents and speech of all the interviewees—from Virginia to Georgia to Texas—appear as if people in those very different regions spoke exactly the same way. The exaggerated dialect was supposed to signal "authenticity," an authenticity defined by incapacity.

Which brings us back to Estebanico, whose sojourn in Texas had taken place nearly a century before the landing at Jamestown, nearly two hundred years before James and Sally Hemings were in France. Estebanico was described as a "black Arab from Azamor," on the coast of Morocco. A Muslim, he had been forced to convert to Christianity and sold away from his home to Spain. He came to the Americas with the man who enslaved him, Andrés Dortantes, one of the leaders of an expedition of three hundred people to Florida, and Cabeza de Vaca. A series of mishaps—a hurricane, illness, and bad encounters with Indigenous people—compelled them to leave Florida. The men split up, and set off by rafts, to cross the Gulf of Mexico.

Estebanico, among around fifty other men on his raft, including Dortantes, made it to Texas, as did Cabeza de Vaca with about fifty or so men on his raft. The three other parties landed farther south and died as a consequence of either Indian attacks or starvation. Estebanico and his party actually made contact with Cabeza de Vaca and the men who had been on his raft. After surviving the trip across the Gulf of Mexico, the elements were against them. The fall turned into a cold and hard winter. Many perished. Over time, Estebanico ended up in a quartet with Cabeza de Vaca and two other men. Their ordeal moved into another phase when they were enslaved by various groups living along the Texas Gulf Coast. The men endured six years in slavery but eventually managed to escape. They then embarked upon an epic journey, walking across Texas to the Pacific Coast (it took years), encountering Native peoples along the way.

Cabeza de Vaca, who lived to produce a wildly popular memoir of the extraordinary adventure, wrote about Estebanico as having played a key role as the chief translator between the Spaniards and the Indigenous people because of his great talent for learning and speaking languages. Estebanico, and the Europeans, became renowned as medicine men by the people they encountered. Estebanico appears to have been able to achieve a measure of respect. That disappeared once he and his fellow wanderers came upon a group of Spaniards in what is now Sonora State in northwestern Mexico. Once they were safe, and back among a strong complement of other Spanairds, Estebanico's Spanish companions were once again in their element.

I don't recall whether Estebanico's talent for languages featured in the fleeting mention that was made of him in my early education. I do wonder what difference it might have made to our understandings about the enslaved to have had a more fully realized example of one who displayed such perseverance and talent. While it is true that Estebanico was not perfect—there were complaints about his treatment of some of the women they encountered, and he ultimately died in a hail of arrows, killed by Indians—even these negative notes would help see him as a human being with strengths and weaknesses. We would have encountered a known person, to substitute for the nameless people in cotton fields who, at least in my education, never broke out and appeared as anything other than fungible agricultural workers. Of course, I know now that the lives of enslaved field-workers were more complicated than portrayed during my childhood, and worshiping heroism, as typically defined, works against the idea that the lives of more common people count and hold lessons for us as well. But learning that the Spanish explorers, and the Indigenous people they encountered and lived with at times, relied on Estebanico to help them speak with one another brings another dimension to our understandings about slavery and the people enslaved.

Even more, knowing that some of the Black people who came to the Americas with the Spanish went off on their own to lead expeditions of conquest in Mexico, Central, and South America would have altered the framework for viewing people of African descent in the New World. Not to place conquering in a good light, but seeing Africans in America who were out of the strict confines of the plantation—and seeing them presented as something other than the metaphorical creation of English people—would have pushed back against the narrative of inherent limitation. Africans were all over the world, doing different things, having all kinds of experiences. Blackness does not equal inherent incapacity and natural limitation.

Over the past several decades, to be sure, academic historians have emphasized very strongly that enslaved people in North America did more than work in the fields. The insights from this scholarship have filtered down to public history sites where enslaved people lived and labored, changing the emphasis of the presentations at those places. If one goes to Williamsburg, Virginia, one sees actors portraying enslaved people who were skilled craftsmen, artisans of one sort or another. At Monticello, guides point out the work of John Hemmings, the carpenter and joiner who made furniture for Jefferson and worked on the physical structure of both Monticello and Poplar Forest, Jefferson's home away from home in Bedford County, ninety miles away from his mountaintop mansion.

As has been said many times, Black history is American history. People of African descent, however, occupy a special place regarding the narrative of the rise and fall of European nations in North America. For all its problems, nationalist-oriented history presented a cogent telling of the origins of the United States, though a superficial one. It made some degree of sense to sunset the influence of the other European nations with whom the Americans contended for control of the continent. American culture continued under the influence of what had been, at the time of the separation, a British society. The critical underpinning of this was the decision to receive the Common Law instead of adopting a system based upon European Civil

Law, making a thing called Anglo-American law that ordered the society in the newly constituted United States.

But would it make sense for African Americans enslaved under English rule to think they had absolutely no connection to enslaved people who spoke Spanish or spoke French? The change in governments was meaningful in certain ways. For example, the Catholic Spanish and French kept records of births and deaths in parish rolls, whereas Protestant denominations generally paid no heed to this. There were other cultural differences. What enslaved Africans had in common, however, what really ordered their lives, was the experience of enslavement in a world in which the notion of White supremacy was ascendant. The echoes of that world have reverberated from the 1500s through to my classrooms in the 1960s and '70s, and continue to reverberate today. There is no reason for the people taken from Africa to define themselves strictly by the categories their captors created. Even though the Spanish "lost" Texas and Florida, Estebanico and the Spanish-speaking Blacks of St. Augustine should be seen as a part of the origin story of African Americans. These people, all but a handful of whom were brought to different parts of the New World for one purpose, are related to one another no matter their language or religion.

As a matter of fact, a closer look at the story of the twenty or so Africans who landed at Jamestown contains a hint of the broader nature of the origin story, for the Africans, from the region of Angola, had been taken after a battle with a Spanish galleon. They had Spanish names that were later anglicized once they settled into the Virginia colony. The Spanish, and their Portuguese neighbors, had been enslaving Africans, working with elites within African societies, for centuries by this time. The English were relative newcomers to the practice. The field of Atlantic history, which studies the era of contact between Africans, Europeans, and Indigenous people in the sixteenth through eighteenth centuries, began to take hold in the 1980s, when I was in college and in law school. It has expanded further, as a challenge to inward-looking nationalist history. Thinking of these interactions as part of a global system makes even more clear that the origin story of Africans in North America is much richer and more complicated than the story of twenty Africans arriving in Jamestown in 1619. The story, with all its aspects and components, had even earlier origins in the region that would become Texas.

People of the Past and the Present

When I was growing up, Six Flags Over Texas was a dream destination for me and all the kids I knew. I had one group of friends in the small town where I lived and another in the even smaller town where I was born, the home of my grandparents, which we visited nearly every weekend and where I spent part of the summer. We were used to the traveling carnivals that showed up periodically with concession stands, Ferris wheels, and rides of one sort or another that thrilled, or just made us sick. From all that we had heard, the still-new Six Flags, which had opened in 1961, was a much bigger deal than anything I had experienced before, different in a way that excited the imagination. First, it was in a far-off place—Dallas (actually Arlington, outside of Dallas) around two hundred miles north of where we lived. We understood it was one of the two "Big City" counterpoints to nearby Houston. The other was San Antonio, or San Antone, as some relatives in my grandparents' generation called it, in a way that suggested to my young ears, worldly inside knowledge. I liked hearing them say it. San Antonio, the smallest of the three, was just bit farther away from my hometown than Dallas, but it seemed even more remote, farther to the West, with no gigantic theme park and, most important for me, no known cousins who would have made it a destination for my family. For these reasons, the city was pretty much off my radar screen.

But we had cousins in Dallas, and there was Six Flags Over Texas, which we children always referred to by its full name. *Can we go to Six Flags Over Texas?* Or, *I'm going to Six Flags Over Texas!* Even today, as the franchise has moved around the country, when I hear people say "Six Flags," my mind fills in "Over Texas" and I have to resist the temptation to explain why "Six Flags." The six flags refer to the six flags of the countries that flew over Texas in history: Spain, France, Mexico, the Republic of Texas, the United States, and the Confederate States of America. I have no idea if it's the same way now, but the original park had sections that depicted Texas's time under each particular flag, a conceit that would make less sense as the franchise expanded to places outside of Texas that had no similar multinational history.

I don't remember what year it was, but it was likely around the time I was in kindergarten or first grade that I made my first, and only trip, to Six Flags Over Texas. I don't know what the occasion was for the outing. It must have been the summer, because a girl who typically visited her aunt (our neighbor) for stretches of time in the summer, the way I visited my grandparents, came along with us. I believe the trip, by bus, was under the auspices of some of the people who, along with my mother, taught at Booker T. Washington High School. It would likely have been the first time I had been on a commercial bus, and I remember the then-unfamiliar sounds of the bus brakes as they came to rest, and the sharp scent of gasoline in the dimly lit loading area as we boarded.

The trip to Six Flags was an all-Black affair, of which I remember little save for two things, besides boarding the bus to get there: It was my first time seeing a toucan, like the one in the then–still relatively new cereal Froot Loops. I distinctly remember saying hello to the bird, thinking that it might, like a parrot and the bird on TV, be able to talk. Alas, it could not. You have to remember, I was very young. The other thing I recall was the rescue of one of the children who came on the trip; the girl who visited her aunt every year. We were in a section that had a walkway with water on one side. She was directly in front of me, chatting away with great animation when she looked up at her aunt and said, "Auntie . . ." and then in a grand misstep walked straight into the water. In a fraction of a second, a very pale young man, with light brown hair, wearing what was supposed to be the garb of an Indian—buckskin pants, no shirt, war paint, with a headdress that signaled to my young self "Indian Brave," a headband with a single feather—executed a perfect dive into the water to retrieve her. His straightened body put me in mind of an expertly tossed spear. Never before, or since, have I seen a quicker response. The whole thing had the air of a synchronized dance. She stepped into the water, and he followed near-simultaneously without missing a beat. I don't remember what era of Texas we were supposed to be in, but the young man, whom I took to be a White man dressed as an Indian, was there prepared for just such a mishap.

Although it is conceivable that the rescuer was part Native American—I know now that appearance alone doesn't answer that question—I was certain, then, that he was White because of the way he looked. Also, because, even at the young age, I had gotten the message that Indians were part of the past. They had once been in Texas, but were there no longer; the same could be said for the country overall. Whatever quaint depiction of Texas this young man was dressed to be a part of, it reinforced the idea of current absence. The television shows I saw that featured Indians—and we were still in the era of TV westerns, original shows and reruns of older shows—were all about an American past that no longer existed. There may have been some, but I don't recall television shows in which Indians appeared as characters in contemporary situations. At this point in my young life, there were Black people and White people in Texas, with Mexicans, as I would have identified them, in some other parts of the state.

The depictions of Indigenous people were very much about fitting Texas into the western frontier. The childhood game "Cowboys and Indians" emphasized conflict, and we were always clear about the way that real conflict turned out: the Indians occasionally won battles but lost the ultimate war. Conceptualizing Texas as the western frontier helped tell the story of the region's past as a form of "winners'" history. The only Native peoples who really mattered were ones with whom White settlers had come into the greatest conflict: Comanches and Apaches. Consequently, these were the two groups I remember hearing the most about. That makes sense, at some level, as these intense interactions formed a part of White Texans' story of how they came to live in and dominate that space.

Having "won" the territory by force, which rightly creates at least some degree of unease in a society in which the maxim "might makes right" is ostensibly rejected, and used to critique people who believe that force alone justifies outcomes, the story of conquest had to be leavened with examples of cooperation and, even, intermixture between the contending forces in the state. In Texas history classes, we learned the story of Quanah Parker, the son of Peta Nocona, a Comanche chief and Cynthia Ann Parker, who had been kidnapped from her Anglo-American family when she was between eight and eleven years old—the

exact year of her birth is unknown. The Parkers had come
to Texas from Illinois, settling on the frontier leading into
the land of the Comanches. They cleared land and built
a fort, understanding that they would likely come under
attack, as they were settling in an area that others claimed
as well. Sure enough, in 1836, the Comanches attacked the
fort, killing some members of the family and taking others,
including Cynthia, along with them. By 1840, Cynthia,
who had been given the name Na-ura, was married off to
Peta Nocona.

Members of her family who survived the raid spent
years working for her return. On two occasions, Whites
made contact with her and tried to bring her back to her
family. The Comanches refused to release her, and Parker
herself declined to return to the White community. Finally,
twenty-four years after she had been taken, she was unwill-
ingly brought back to her family. By then she had had three
children, only one of whom, Quanah, survived long after
her return. Parker died around 1870, apparently still in dis-
tress at having been forced to leave the only life she had
known since childhood. Her son Quanah grew up to be
called the "last of the Comanche chiefs." He was a skilled
military leader, besting Whites in many battles. In the end,
when it became apparent that his people could no longer
sustain themselves through hunting buffalo, he surrendered, agreeing to move, along with his group, to a reservation in Oklahoma in 1875.

I don't remember whether I first heard of Quanah Parker in fourth-grade Texas history or seventh-grade Texas history. There may have been two iterations of the story, appropriate for the different age groups. Perhaps that's why it has stuck with me. That, and the fact it seemed to me that so many wrong things were packed into this one narrative, things that implicated broad and narrow topics. On the broad side, even then, I had an instinctive sympathy for people who were being forced off of land they considered their province. Frankly, that the people who were doing the forcing were also the people who had held Black people in slavery deepened my sympathy, seeing in my mind that there should have been an affinity between Blacks and Indigenous people in those times.

My father, who loved Westerns, and always rooted for the Indians in television shows and films, almost certainly influenced my view. He, too, made the connection between Whites' enslavement of Blacks and Whites' forcing Indians off the land. How could he not? Land taken from Native peoples in Texas was then cleared by enslaved people, who were then put to work planting, tending, and harvesting crops. There was, also, some degree of romanticizing what he took to be the lives of Indigenous people. When he was a boy, he had a tendency to play hooky. The rituals of school bored him. His exasperated father (he'd lost his mother at age eleven) would escort him to school. My father would walk in the front door, wait a moment until his father continued on to work, and then walk out the back door. He would go back home, get on his horse, and ride off into the woods to read books, something he loved to do, and often hunt. Perhaps he thought he was living, at least somewhat, like an Indian. Indeed, the identification was so strong that he apparently told one of my brothers that he had some Indian ancestry. I supposed anything is possible—there were Native peoples in Texas and in Georgia, where my father's family was said to have originated. But I was skeptical and was stunned to hear he had said that because I knew he preferred to think of himself as of 100 percent African origin, and he would tease my mother because she had some White ancestry.

I don't know if my father knew it, and had mentally pushed it into the background, but I certainly didn't yet know that relations between enslaved African Americans and Indians were not as I thought they should have been. It would be years before I learned that the so-called Five Civilized Tribes—Cherokee, Chickasaw, Choctaw, Creek, and Seminole—had enslaved Black people, that some Native people held (and hold) the same racist attitude toward Black people that many Whites do. There was no "natural" alliance. This displays very well the contingent nature of history, and how difficult it can be, when considering the history of a given time and place, to keep in mind that our view is colored by the knowledge of how things turned out. Writers, and consumers, of history must take great care not to import the knowledge we have into the minds of people and of circumstances in the past. That is different from recognizing points of connection between the past and the present. It is more about wishful thinking about the past.

I could believe that Indians and African Americans and, actually different Indians among themselves, *should* have recognized that they faced a common foe. But that is because I had imbibed the racial thinking of my times, which had largely been imposed by Europeans—creating people called "white" and categories of people who were "nonwhite" for purposes of deciding what rights people had and how they could be treated or mistreated. As a measure of self-defense, African Americans went with that program, and forged ties based on race, making a positive out of what had been created as a negative. All of that was in the big picture of the Parker narrative, a story of encroachment, met by defense and retaliation. Actually, that story was bigger and older than Whites versus Indians. The Comanches themselves were not indigenous to Texas, having come to the area from more northern regions of what we know as the United States, displacing, most often with violence, other native groups as they went. Over time, they created what has been called an "empire," the Comancheria, that extended through parts of Kansas, Oklahoma, New Mexico, Texas, and into northern Mexico. The picture was, indeed, bigger and more complicated than I imagined during my childhood.

There was also the smaller, more intimate, story of a child, who was around the same age as I would have been in either fourth- or seventh-grade Texas history. Cynthia Ann Parker was still a girl, and she had been taken from her family against her will. It made sense that the nearly two and half decades away from the Parkers made a huge difference to her thinking and personality. But I could not, then, imagine ever forgetting my mother and family by the time I had reached the age Cynthia Parker was when she was taken. And the notion that she had been "adopted" into a group of people who had kidnapped her from her family didn't sit well with me. I was a proceduralist from an early age—how things happened, how they were done, mattered. I couldn't wrap my mind around the idea that "adoption" into the group who had forcibly removed her from her family could be seen as in any way mitigating the wrongness of what had happened to her.

Remembering the presentation of the story today, that Parker ultimately did not want to go back to the White community, influenced the way people viewed the story. It was also, likely, significant that she was said to have told people she loved Nocona and that he was said to have loved her, as evidenced by his failure to ever take another wife, which he could have. There was also, no doubt, the adult realization that life is not fair; a reality that kids have to learn. There was no way to undo what had happened in 1836. People, meaning Parker, had to carry on. But we don't know how that equanimity about life with her kidnappers was achieved. I get the distinct impression that the prominence of Parker's husband and son shaped the presentation of how she ended up as part of the Comanche community in the first place. Parker's life is judged by the men to whom she was attached: a powerful and important husband and a powerful and important son. That she was kidnapped is fine because she married well. How would the story have been viewed if a less important male in the group had taken the thirteen- or fourteen-year-old as a wife, and she had had no children, daughters, or a son who did not grow up to become a famous leader? It's almost certain that her story would not likely have been told to us more than just in passing in our history class.

The gender issues in the story certainly were not a part of our consideration. It would be interesting to know how younger generations view Cynthia Parker's life story, especially generations coming of age during the past two years with the heightened concern about issues of consent, sexual predation, and sexual assault. Whether the Comanches accepted her or not, and whatever sympathy we have for a people under siege and fighting for their very existence, there is no way to minimize the problem with kidnapping girls to make them brides. That has happened throughout history on every continent, belonging to the days when women's autonomy was devalued and when they were considered as property.

Although the Comanches and Apaches dominated my earliest imagination of Indian life in Texas history, the reality is that people lived in the area long before either of the two groups arrived. During the Ice Age, Native peoples came to a region in the Panhandle of Texas to quarry Alibates flint, a type of stone used to make tools and arrowheads. Because of its significance, the site was the first in Texas to be designated a national monument, now only one of three in the state. Later, permanent villages were formed in the area. Farther south in what is now Texas, there is also evidence of other early settlements. Indigenous people were all over the area. Later peoples included the Caddos, a farming group who lived in the pine forests of East Texas and called their confederacy Te-Haas, rendered Tejas by the Spanish, which was the Caddo word for "the friends." That is thought to be the origin of the word "Texas."

By seventh grade, I knew first hand that my earlier assumption that Indians were only a part of Texas's past was wrong. In fact, some were never far away from me. About seventeen miles from the hospital where I was born is the reservation of the Alabama-Coushattas, set on just over 10,000 acres. Like the Comanches, the Alabama-Coushattas had migrated to Texas, though without building anything that could be described as an empire. The Alabamas (from the chiefdom Alibamu in Alabama) and the Coushattas (from the Coste chiefdom, speaking the language Koasati, in southern Tennessee) were distinct groups who have long been associated with one another, sharing a similar language and culture. They both descended from people who in the Mississippian period of 1000 to 1600 dominated the area that is now the southeastern part of the United States. Their languages are branches from a common Muskogean language tree. When Hernando de Soto arrived to explore Florida in 1539 looking for gold, he began a process that would transform the region and the lives of the people who were already living there. The Coushattas first encountered him in July of 1540, the Alabamas later in November of that same year.

There are no written records of the events, oral history suggests that the conflict and disease brought by the Spanish caused significant disruption in the lives of the Alabamas and Coushattas, the same story that played out in other areas where Indigenous people had contact with Europeans. This, even as other more powerful Native groups were raiding both Coushattas and Alabamas, capturing members and selling them to traders in the Carolinas. By the beginning of 1700s, the two groups had formed an alliance, though there is no set answer as to why. Both groups had moved to an area near present-day Montgomery, Alabama. The similarity of their language allowed them to communicate, and their shared customs, and intermarriage, made it easy for them to live jointly. After their consolidation, having been victims themselves, they participated in what was a newly expanded trade in Indian slaves.

As happened to Cynthia Parker's family, taking people from other groups, most often women and children, was a common act of warfare. Indeed, the capacity to success-fully raid was a show of strength. But the English desire for Indian slaves who could be sold to the West Indies spurred the market in human beings, transforming the practice and destabilizing southeastern societies overall. Captured peo-ple were now commodities. And, as happened all over the colonies in North America, the Alabama-Coushattas were drawn into European balance-of-power politics among the English, French, and Spanish. We think our society is uniquely complicated today, but it is hard to fathom this world of colliding cultures, languages, religions, differen-tials of power—with few restraints on how power could be deployed—all of this taking place when people had no understanding of, or capability to deal with, the even greater powers in their world: bacteria and viruses.

The Alabamas and Coushattas began to leave Ala-bama to migrate farther west in the 1760s to get away from turmoil that had visited their homeland. Their westward migration is part of a metaphorical origin story called the "Journey to the Sky" that has three Alabama-Coushatta boys traveling west because they wanted to see exactly where the sun set. The group continued west, settling first in what is now Louisiana and then East Texas beginning in the 1780s and on into the first two decades of the nine-teenth century. The group joined a rich cultural mixture of other groups of Indians, Tejanos, Whites, and Blacks. They farmed, and sold produce in the Spanish market.

This was not at all a stable situation for the group. In addition to battling the Comanches, the Alabama-Coushattas got involved on the side of Mexicans in their war for independence from Spain, which resulted in Mexican recognition of their rights to hold land in East Texas. But that settlement was short-lived. Later, when the Texians and Tejanos sought independence from Mexico, the Alabamas and Coushattas negotiated an agreement with revolutionary leader Sam Houston. Under the terms of the deal, the Republic of Texas, if it came into being, would guarantee that it recognized the groups' right to their land, if they agreed not to side with Mexico in the conflict. As the conflict unfolded, the group also aided White settlers fleeing from Antonio López de Santa Anna, president of Mexico and victorious general at the famed Battle of the Alamo.

After the republic had been achieved, however, other Texians balked at the deal, saying that all of Texas should be available to White settlers. Houston had envisioned a plan for peaceful coexistence with Indians. The man who took office after him, Mirabeau B. Lamar, a Georgia transplant and poet, had a different idea. He wanted any Indigenous people who fought Whites to be annihilated. Other Indians would be forced to leave Texas or be settled on reservations designated for them by the republic. It was not until ten years after Texas had become part of the United States that the Alabama-Coushattas found a permanent home. Largely because their numbers had been reduced, because they had no powerful allies, and because they had aided Texas revolutionaries, Lamar exempted them from his genocidal policies. Sam Houston supported the Texas legislature's move to give the Alabamas a little over 1,000 acres of land near the town where I was born. A year later, the Coushattas were given land, but much of it was claimed by Whites. Many of them stayed on the land given to the Alabamas, who welcomed them. They, in effect, became one people in Texas's Big Thicket.

I knew nothing about this history when I started visiting the reservation in my preteen years and afterward. The "Indian Reservation" was a place to go to see a culture that was different from the one that I was used to, Black and White. It was also a place to take people who came to Livingston to visit my grandparents when my family was there. Sometimes cousins came along. This was in the days before gaming on the reservation, an activity that has had an enormous impact on the surrounding community, making the reservation one of the largest employers in Polk County. I remember a simpler affair, a small village-like atmosphere, a campground, and stores to buy Native American paraphernalia—small bags, ties, bracelets, necklaces.

In the 1970s, these types of items were very much sought after. We started going to the reservation during the height of the American Indian Movement. Popular culture was full of Native American–related themes and imagery. High-profile events from the superserious—the incident at Wounded Knee, which resulted in deaths—to the symbolic—Marlon Brando's sending a Native American woman to decline the Oscar he won for his portrayal of Don Corleone in the 1972 film *The Godfather*—drew attention to Native peoples. A public service announcement from that era, designed to combat littering, featured an Indian man (the actor Iron Eyes Cody, who was actually Sicilian) in full dress walking through a modern United States covered in litter. In the final frame, he sheds a single tear.

All of this fit with the hippie-themed back-to-the-land movement that romanticized Indigenous people as much as taking them seriously. It was also of a piece with earlier responses to Native Americans. After removing them from their land, preventing them from becoming a threat, Americans often claimed to admire the special virtues of Native peoples, who were supposed to possess a unique spirit. They named towns after them, states, later sports franchises. That iconic commercial with the "Crying Indian" played to the idea that Indigenous people have a spiritual connection to the land that others do not possess. The people who took their land did not appreciate it, or care for it properly. This was almost a half-hearted confession that what had happened was wrong. That didn't mean the land would be given back to them, of course.

This idea of a heightened Indian sensibility, or spiri-

tuality, flowed through a movie series that was something
of a phenomenon in my hometown in the 1970s—Tom
Laughlin's *Billy Jack* franchise. The title character was a
half-White, half–Native American man. Adding to this
supposedly potent mixture was another cultural obsession
of the 1970s—martial arts, of which Billy Jack was a master. *"Everybody was Kung Fu Fighting."* This may not have
played as well in other parts of the country, but, impor-
tantly, for my hometown, Billy Jack was a veteran, and
not just any kind, but a former member of an elite force,
the Green Berets. Everything about the character's basic
makeup—down to his DNA—telegraphed that he was the
good guy.

The movie was set in a small town full of close-minded
conservative White people who were hostile to the students
and director of the Freedom School, whose name hints at
the school's ethos and why the townspeople hated it so. It
was a hippie school, run by Jean Roberts, played by Delores
Taylor, the real-life spouse of Tom Laughlin. It had students of all colors, and was on an Indian reservation. Jack
and Roberts had some connection that I couldn't quite figure, as I don't remember them acting openly as lovers. Trou-
ble ensued whenever the students came into town. These
encounters often ended with Billy Jack using his martial-
arts skills to dispatch the town wrongdoer, usually to the
applause of the theater audience. When the movie's chief
villain sexually assaults Jean Roberts, kills a Native Amer-

ican student, and tries to kill Billy Jack, Jack kills him. A standoff with the police ends when Roberts talks Billy Jack into surrendering. As he is taken away, his supporters line the roads with lifted clenched fists, another gesture from the 1970s, that, I confess, I found thrilling and moving.

It struck me then, but not as much as now, how odd it was that people in my hometown loved this movie, and the sequel. The theater was invariably packed with people who seemed to identify with, and feel protective toward, the characters associated with the school. Yet, the majority of people in the audience, at least on the surface, had more in common with the townspeople in the movie than the hippies of the Freedom School. That was my perspective, but I would have been one of a small number of Black people in the movie theater, since the Black population in Conroe hovered around 7 percent during that time. We were very much in the minority.

More likely, it was the character Billy Jack with whom they identified. The half-Indian martial arts master and Green Beret had decided to protect the hippies. His support gave my fellow townspeople permission to identify with, and champion, characters who in real life many of them would have disdained. That he was part White also made him safe. Would the appeal have been as great if the character had been a full-blooded Native American? Could audience members have lost themselves in such a character so thoroughly, giving themselves permission to imagine themselves as a non-White person? Certainly, the people who made movies during those days would have wondered about that. It was an article of faith in Hollywood that White audiences were not keen on watching films with people of color as the main characters. That common wisdom has been exploded in the past few decades.

It was also important that the film presented right and wrong in extremely broad strokes. Billy Jack's purity, proved by his Native heritage, helped make the choices very clear to my fellow townspeople, who undoubtedly saw the movie differently than I. The townspeople on the screen looked awfully like some people I knew in Conroe and Livingston. I have no way of knowing the answer, but I wonder if any of them made the connection between the racial intolerance—the lack of tolerance for difference, in general—displayed in the film and the forms of intolerance that had been a part of our town.

Perhaps sitting in the dark, out of easy sight of their neighbors, allowed them to give vent to sympathies that they could not express openly. I had observed, very early on, that Whites policed one another on racial matters, like my White classmates who were friendly at school but acted differently when we saw each other out of that context, when they were with their families or other friends. My father insisted that this policing went on, that my White friends could know the right thing to do—even want to do it—but could not bring themselves to do it because they feared losing the love, esteem, and support of their community. It was never just a matter of individual feelings or weaknesses. My father did not use the term, but he was suggesting the problem was structural.

Or, perhaps, the audience simply liked the violence, watching a morality play that could be taken just at surface level, with no need for angst-ridden self-reflection. *Billy Jack* fit perfectly into the formula of a Western, with which the audience was familiar. The man of few words, and much action, who protected the people around him against the bad guys. This time the Cowboy and the Indian had merged to create a hero that my fellow townspeople could accept. They would have no reason to go beyond that, while I was trying to make sense of the experience of being a form of outsider, like the kids in the Freedom School, in a place I had lived in since I was six months old.

By the time I had left home for Dartmouth, a school started in 1769 to educate Native Americans, the visits to the Alabama-Coushatta Indian Reservation had ceased. I cherished the items I had bought there. But my teenaged interests were elsewhere. My brothers, both older, had left home. The cousins gathered less frequently, and my grandparents were older and not so inclined to make the trip. In the twenty-first century, the United States has come to a point of reckoning about its past, including the story of the dispossession of Native peoples, who are still very much present. At the same time where appropriate, Native peo-

ples are now being asked to come to grips with their relationship to African Americans, the descendants of people
whom they enslaved, and with whom, in some cases, they
share a bloodline. The American story is, indeed, endlessly
complicated.

Remember the Alamo

"One ever feels his twoness,—an American, a Negro; two souls, two thoughts, two unreconciled strivings; two warring ideals in one dark body, whose dogged strength alone keeps it from being torn asunder." With those famous words, W. E. B. Du Bois, in his masterpiece *The Souls of Black Folk*, identifies the central dilemma facing Black people in the United States—that, to a great degree, "Blackness" and "Americanness" have been cast in opposition to one another, a predicament created by the details of history and the desires of others. What has it meant (what does it mean) for Blacks to claim Americanness while substantial numbers of their fellow Americans reject the idea that Blacks can be true Americans? And that they have used their greater numbers to make that rejection the basis of law and social policy?

When Du Bois wrote that in 1903, he had every reason to focus on Black double consciousness. The country was not yet a decade beyond the Supreme Court case *Plessy v. Ferguson*, which said that as a matter of official policy, when it came to matters of race, the United States could move on "separate but equal" tracks, even though it was obvious to all that the "separate" facilities, schools, and the like, created for Black people were not "equal." There could be first-class citizenship and second-class citizenship in the American republic. The "twoness," then, was externally imposed and, as always in history, a different path could have been taken. Almost from the very beginning of their time in North America, Blacks have shown their deep and patriotic attachment to the country they helped to build, even as they have been utterly realistic about the way many of their fellow countrymen viewed them. Persisting in the face of that reality has been a struggle of centuries.

What are we then to make of Black Texans, who may feel the "twoness" Du Bois described when thinking about their status as Americans, but also have to confront the same double consciousness when considering their place in Texas. This may be yet another instance of making Texas "exceptional"—and again turning it into a small version of an "exceptional" United States—when residents of other states may be in a similar position. African Americans in all the states of the former Confederacy, just for example, are potentially in the position of loving a place that was deeply oppressive to their ancestors. What sane Black person could feel nostalgia for the so-called "Golden Age of Virginia," the period from the 1730s to the 1760s? Texas has, however, pushed itself into national and international consciousness in a way that only one other place in the United States— New York City, or perhaps California—can match. So, Texans are not believing things about their exceptionalism (in a good way or bad way) all by themselves. The image keeps returning to them in an endless feedback loop.

My first conscious memory of thinking about Texas as a distinct place was of a tragedy. While I was visiting my grandparents' house, President John F. Kennedy was assassinated in Dallas, Texas. I remember the wails of a woman on the grounds of Paul Laurence Dunbar High School, which was across the street from where my grandparents lived. I could tell from the conversation of the adults around me that their regret that this had happened—and had happened in Texas—was profound.

The television was on all the time in those tragic days, bringing news of events as they unfolded. I recall standing before it in the living room while my grandmother was in the kitchen cooking. We were the only people in the house on that Sunday morning. I saw men, wearing the same kind of Stetson hat my father wore, escorting Lee Harvey Oswald. And then, suddenly, he was shot. For a split second, I was deeply confused. It seemed unreal. *Did that happen?* I had seen people shot on television, but only in dramas and Westerns. Make-believe. But this was supposed to be real. *Can people really be shot on TV?* Living in the world of childhood, asking for permission to do things, having things proceed in an orderly fashion, I couldn't fathom how this could have happened. I've watched the tape of those moments as an adult. Even though I am much more aware of the unpredictability of life, and have the knowledge of hindsight that this *did* happen, the moment still feels a bit unreal.

I was not old enough to think of the events in Dallas as fitting into any broader pattern of Texas history or culture. It was a violent act, and it was clear to me that everyone in my world experienced it as a deep and senseless tragedy. I did not know it at the time, but some number of my fellow Texans didn't see it that way at all. They welcomed Kennedy's violent death because they violently disagreed with his politics. The idea of violence as a solution to a problem has plagued humankind from the beginning. People all over the world have employed violence to move situations from one point to another. But there is no question that violence has been at the heart of the Texas story, or I should say violence has been foregrounded in the origin stories of Texas, in ways it is not in other states. Perhaps this is related to my statement that the image of Texas is of a White male, and males are more prone to violence. Certainly, Hollywood has helped this along, contributing to the feedback loop mentioned above. Texas is firmly within the Western movie genre, and there is no similar genre associated with the East, North, and South. Even without the Western theme, with its sheriffs, gunfighters, and outlaws, people had to fight in, and for, Texas.

In 1967, there was a re-release of the 1960 film *The Alamo*. I was taken to see it with my best friend, a boy of my same age who lived next door. This was the year before we took fourth-grade history, but we knew who all the major characters in the movie (real-life people) were before we even went to see the movie. I knew Jim Bowie had a knife, and rather than just being a type of knife he became famous for using in a fight that gained lots of publicity—a knife that others were able to buy and use, too—I imbued it with almost magical properties. This shows the extent to which the story of that iconic place was present in the lives of even young Texans. Bowie and David "Davy" Crockett, of course, were famous nationwide before the movie first appeared. Disney had made Crockett famous in a television miniseries in the 1950s. I can't imagine that as many kids were familiar with William Barret Travis, the commandant at the Alamo, and Santa Anna, the general of the Mexican army and president of Mexico.

Not much about the film remains with me other than my friend's reaction to the moment when it was apparent that any battle to control the Alamo, an old Spanish mission turned into a fort, would be futile. The man who had been charged with holding the Alamo, Colonel Travis, played by the dashing Laurence Harvey, his English accent barely disguised, delivers the speech to the assembled group letting them know that reinforcements were not on the way. Travis asks the men to choose their fates, assuring them that no one could fairly criticize them if they left. In Texas legend, Travis actually drew a line in the sand with his sword to indicate that all who stepped over it would be on his side. At the end of the speech, and as the men, who were not real soldiers, but volunteers, dismounted and walked to Travis's side, I glanced toward my friend to see tears streaming down his face. He was deeply moved to see this show of loyalty even in the face of death.

I also recalled being slightly embarrassed by the character who was Jim Bowie's slave. I knew by then to flinch, or slightly hold my breath even, whenever Black actors appeared in movies, especially old films. I never knew what was going to happen, but I knew what *could* happen. Would the Black character be good for Black people, or bad for Black people? I had a strong sense that such things could never just be about that one actor's characterization. There were so few representations of Blacks in films in those days that every appearance counted. Television was a bit ahead of the game on this. Movies, an early (and continuing) delight, may have been generally fraught when Blacks appeared, but not those with Sidney Poitier, even the ones made before I was born that ran on television. I could relax, even become exhilarated, when he came on screen. I knew everything would be just right.

Although the names of the heroes of the Alamo were

already known to me, I didn't know that an enslaved person was there. I knew about slavery and that it would not have been unusual for Bowie to have an enslaved personal servant. In fact, it was Colonel Travis who brought an enslaved manservant, named Joe, with him to the Alamo. The enslaved person attached to Bowie was a woman, his cook, Betty. There were other enslaved people in the mission. None of these people had the unfettered choice to remain on the other side of Travis's line in the sand. I don't recall if Travis's enslaved manservant appeared in the movie. Given that Travis was a powerful Texian, I wouldn't have been surprised if his manservant had been depicted. I did not know the extent of the real-life Bowie's involvement with slavery, that he had been born in Kentucky and grew up in Louisiana in a household with enslaved workers, that he inherited enslaved people from his father and, later, made his living trading enslaved people, working with his brother and the notorious pirate Jean Lafitte on various slave-smuggling schemes. The men bought a plantation, ran it for a while, and then sold it for a great profit. Bowie then moved to Texas, where he renounced his American citizenship and became a Mexican citizen to reap the advantages given to citizens over mere residents and married into a prominent Tejano family. However, he soon became sympathetic to the move for Texas independence. That is how he ended up in the Alamo.

The main point conveyed in the movie, and in my history classes, was that the men who fought and died at the

Alamo did so for a noble cause: occupying the Mexican army until Sam Houston could organize his forces. This was part of the war for Texas independence, which was an unquestionably good thing. Who could not want Texas to be independent? The movie was centered on the siege and the battle in which Mexicans triumphed. All was not lost. The memory of the gallant men who sacrificed their lives there, and the memory of Texian prisoners of war who had been massacred at Goliad not long after the Alamo, gave rise to the exhortations "Remember the Alamo!," "Remember Goliad!" That was the battle cry of Texian and Tejano fighters as the Battle of San Jacinto began under the command of General Sam Houston. They scored a decisive victory. Santa Anna's forces retreated. He was captured a few days later, and while he was held hostage signed a treaty ("That was under duress. That *couldn't* be legal," my father insisted when we talked about this years after I saw the movie) agreeing to the removal of all Mexican troops from Texas. With no Mexican military forces in place, Texas could become, or at least act as if it were, independent.

The Texians were ready for independence. Even before the fall of the Alamo, delegates had met at Washington-on-the-Brazos and drafted a Texas Declaration of Independence that is essentially a knockoff of Jefferson's American Declaration—pronouncements, followed by a list of grievances. What the Texas Declaration very pointedly does not take from Jefferson are any words about "self-evident" truth that "all men are created equal." There was no place for such language in a battle in which race and culture were central. General Provisions of the Constitution, also drafted in this intense period, make concerns about controlling people of color, protecting slavery, and managing the new republic's racial future very clear.

> SEC. 6. All free white persons who shall emigrate to this republic, and who shall, after a residence of six months, make oath before some competent authority that he intends to reside permanently in the same, and shall swear to support this Constitution, and that he will bear true allegiance to the republic of Texas, shall be entitled to all the privileges of citizenship.

In the new republic, only Whites were welcome.

> SEC. 9. All persons of color who were slaves for life previous to their emigration to Texas, and who are now held in bondage, shall remain in the like state of servitude: *provided*, The said slave shall be the bona-fide property of the person so holding said slave as aforesaid. Congress shall pass no laws to prohibit emigrants from bringing their slaves into the republic with them, and holding them by the same tenure by which such slaves were held in the United States; nor shall congress have power to emancipate slaves; nor shall

any slaveholder be allowed to emancipate his or her slave or slaves without the consent of congress, unless he or she shall send his or her slave or slaves without the limits of the republic. No free person of African descent, either in whole or in part, shall be permitted to reside permanently in the republic without the consent of congress; and the importation or admission of Africans or negroes into this republic, excepting from the United States of America, is forever prohibited, and declared to be piracy.

Any concerns about the property rights in enslaved people were allayed. Slavery was to be a permanent state for Blacks. This actually interfered with the right to dispose of property as the owner saw fit. Enslavers could not free the people they enslaved without permission.

SEC. 10. All persons, (Africans, the descendants of Africans, and Indians excepted,) who were residing in Texas on the day of the declaration of independence, shall be considered citizens of the republic, and entitled to all the privileges of such . . .

I often encounter great hesitancy about, and impatience with, discussing race when talking about the American past. The obvious difficulty with those kinds of complaints is that people in the past—in the overall American context and in the specific context of Texas—talked a lot about, and did a lot about, race. It isn't some newly discovered fad topic. Race is right there in the documents—official and personal. It would take a concerted effort *not* to consider and analyze the subject, and I realize that evasion is exactly what happened in many of the textbooks that Americans used in their school social studies and history classes. This, in part, accounts for the pained accusations about "revisionist" history when historians talk about things that people had never been made aware of in their history educations.

History is always being revised, as new information comes to light and when different people see known documents and have their own responses to them, shaped by their individual experiences. One person looking, say, at the provision of the Texas Constitution that excluded free Blacks from coming to the state, who does not see that as a problem, or that it had any great implications for the way matters unfolded in what would become the state of Texas, might choose not to discuss the provision at all. Another historian might notice it and wonder how that statement of policy shaped racial relations in the state, perhaps in ways that put the people who lived in the state on a particular path. Not that the path had to have been followed—that's never it—but it is important to know what paths were taken, and why. That is history.

Still, there is no escaping the fact that we humans seem to need myths and legends as well as history. They appear to be an easy way to knit groups of people into a community. That is not a presumptively "feel good" statement. Communities can be held together by positive myths and legends or negative ones. A supreme risk with myths and legends of whatever kind is that we can easily fall in love with the people who are in them, as if we know them. People we actually know come to us with all sorts of good and bad characteristics that become apparent upon repeated contact. We weigh them, sometimes on a daily basis, and determine whether the good outweighs the bad and we wish to continue with the person. That's hard to do with a historical subject, and when it is done through long association, for instance Dumas Malone's over forty-year engagement with Jefferson that produced a six-volume biography, it can approach the kind of intimate knowledge one has with a living being. That knowledge can be transformative. There is a marked difference between Malone's presentation of Jefferson in the first volume, *The Virginian*, published near the end of the 1940s, and the final volume, *The Sage of Monticello*, published near the beginning of the 1980s. By the time he finished work on Jefferson, Malone understood that he was dealing with a far more complex person than he first thought.

Idealizing an individual one doesn't know personally usually involves taking the things one admires and making them embody the individual as a whole. When a historian comes along and says, "Oh, you do know that William

Barret Travis came to Texas one step ahead of the law to avoid being jailed for his debts, abandoning his wife and two small children in the process?," that can be discomfiting. I will freely admit, as realistic about figures in the past as I am, that it disappointed me when I learned of Travis's misdeeds, even though I had no great expectations of him. It was an irrational response, born of the residue of early training about Travis's actions at a particular moment in his life and the life of the state I lived in and, probably, because he was played by Laurence Harvey in the movie *The Alamo*. I can only imagine how a person who was deeply invested in the heroic vision of the leaders of the Alamo might feel. That he left his wife and children under bad circumstances has been given a backstory that suggests, with no real evidence, that his wife, Rosanna, may have had an affair with a neighbor and become pregnant with his child. If we had any reason to think this was true, it might create some smidgen of sympathy for Travis. But, only a smidgen.

The strong available evidence indicates that Travis left behind in Alabama a young mother—she was sixteen when they married—with his two small children, to escape his debts and the arrest warrant that was about to be issued for him. That was not an uncommon course to take in those days. Once in Texas, Travis claimed to be single. He and Rosanna would later be divorced, but they were still married when he first said he was unmarried. And then there is the whole business of Jim Bowie, with his shady deals and slave trading. The answer to this, of course, is that we should refrain from idealizing human beings. We can accept what we think are the good things they did—and there will always be differences of opinion about what "good" means—and not treat them as if they define the entire person. That may be hard to do with myths and legends, but the attempt to recognize and grapple with the humanity and, thus, the fallibility of people in the past—and the present—must be made. That is the stuff of history, too.

One part of the legend of the Alamo that I did not learn during my time in elementary school and William Barret Travis Junior High School was about the "Yellow Rose of Texas." As the story goes, the Texian fighters were able to catch Santa Anna off-guard because he was "distracted" by a "mullato girl" in his tent. There is not much evidence that the president/general was surprised in this way. An Englishman, William Bollaert, who traveled through Texas in the early 1840s, and wrote about the Battle of San Jacinto, made a reference to "a mullato girl belonging to Colonel Morgan" who was in Santa Anna's camp. There was such a person, a woman of color named Emily West, a New Yorker, who was not enslaved. She had signed a contract to be an indentured servant to a man named James Morgan. Because it was hard to imagine that a Black female servant to a White man in Texas could be anything other than enslaved, people assumed she was enslaved, and referred to her as Emily

Morgan. While living in a place called "Morgan's Point," West, and some other servants, were taken by the Mexican army as they pursued David Burnet, the putative president of Texas. Bollaert evidently spoke with people in the area to prepare his writings on San Jacinto. There is some suggestion that "the officer" was none other than General Sam Houston. Bollaert tied West to Santa Anna this way:

> Much has been written relative to this celebrated battle, in which the flower of the Mexican army perished and when Santana was made prisoner, but I beg to introduce the following as given to me by an officer who was engaged in it—given in his own words "The Battle of San Jacinto was probably lost to the Mexicans, owing to the influence of a Mulatta girl (Emily) belonging to Col. Morgan who was closeted in the tent with g'l Satana, at the time the cry was made 'the Enemy! they come! they come! & detained Santana so long, that order could not be restored readily again.'"

Bollaert's journal was not, in fact, published until the mid twentieth century. So, the story of West and Santa Anna, if it lived between the time Bollaert wrote this account and the publication of his journal, lived only in Texas oral history. Over the years, the story changed from being about a woman of color captured by the Mexican army, and forcibly brought to San Jacinto, to a story about a beautiful woman of color who was actually a spy for the Texas revolutionaries, sent by Sam Houston himself to use her great beauty to charm the president of Mexico and top general of the Mexican army on behalf of the Texian revolt. A document does place West at San Jacinto in April of 1836, the month of the battle. Morgan did know Sam Houston, and there is no reason that West, who worked for Morgan, could not have encountered General Houston. At the time of her capture, Morgan was away in Galveston. There is no reason to think, however, that the stories of Houston commissioning her to spy on Santa Anna, and that there was sexual contact between West and Santa Anna, are true. At least one historian has said Santa Anna's stated aversion to interracial mixture would have had made sex with West impossible. That is not a good argument, for reasons well known. And in any event, "had sex" really means "sexually assaulted her," for West was forcibly taken from her home, and she and Santa Anna would not have known each other any length of time.

And the Yellow Rose? The earliest lyrics to the song first appeared in 1853. There is nothing written to suggest that whoever wrote them had Emily West in mind, but they do show that the song was indeed about a woman of color.

> *There's a yellow girl in Texas*
> *That I'm going down to see*
> *No other darkies know her*

No darkey, only me
She cried so when I left her
That it like to broke my heart,
And if I only find her
we never more will part

Even without the self-identification "darkey," it should be obvious that a song about a "yellow girl" would be about a woman of color, whether this was based on Emily West or not. Referring to a White woman as "yellow" would hardly have been seen as a compliment in 1853. Everyone would know it would be saying that she was part African, a thing that was seen by Whites as defamatory. At least since the eighteenth century, the word "yellow" was commonly used to describe people of mixed African and European ancestry. Minstrelsy is by definition over the top. Along with the thrill of using a derogatory term for a Black person, putting the word "darkey" in the song also provided a form of psychic cover for White men who wanted to sing it. It wouldn't do for a White man to sing about his personal longing for a "yellow girl." Indeed, by the twentieth century, the "yellow girl" had disappeared, replaced by the "yellow rose," a non-racial phrase that appeared in a later stanza in the original song. Of course, "darkey" was out, too.

More fascinating than whether this somewhat banal story connecting West to Santa Anna is true—banal because of the stock character of the beautiful exotic temptress who virtually hypnotizes a powerful man into helplessness—is the question that the cultural studies people would ask, "What work is this story doing?" Was it first intended as a slap at interracial mixture, a cautionary tale about a man of European origin brought low by his attraction to a non-White woman? Or was it a way to suggest the innate degeneracy of Texas's great foe, and all Mexicans: at the moment the battle was joined, he was having sex with a "yellow girl"? The story about Houston sending West to Santa Anna plays on a stereotype about African-American women. That West would accept the assignment, and carry it out, suggests her natural licentiousness. Why would West care that much about the Texas Revolution? Her time in the area would have given her a picture of race relations. It's doubtful that would have made her a devoted revolutionary for Texas. She would not even be able to live in the Republic as it was to be constituted. And Houston wouldn't send a reputable White woman to have sex with Santa Anna. Nor would the story of his having done so redound to his credit.

Whatever the reason, the story of Emily West's connection to the Alamo was not one that would have fit in either my fourth- or seventh-grade Texas history classes, or have been discussed much in other venues. The sexual aspect of it would have kept the story underground. I know exactly how my fourth-grade friends would have handled the story if they had heard about—John and Brett in particular. They were just learning how to curse. My seventh-grade cohort may have handled it better. The taboo about interracial sex would certainly have made it more radioactive. Even though, it's safe to say, few people in my school and town—Black or White—would have thought of Santa Anna as White, but he was still different enough from Emily West to make things uncomfortable. Sending the message that Sam Houston thought this was okay would not have been on the table.

In truth, I don't recall hearing anything about the story of West and Santa Anna until I was on a trip home to Conroe in the 1990s to visit my family. By then, I had my own children. It surprised me. But one thing that has changed greatly in Texas from my childhood up until now is the determination to bring people of color into the Texas narrative as much as possible. That is all to the good, and a thing that can be done as a matter of course in researching and writing history. There is material to be gathered in the archives, and there are new ways to approach the material that is already known. The chief difficulty lies in how people of color can be fit into the legends and myths about Texas when the actual historical experiences of Indians, Blacks, and Mexicans wreak havoc with those legends and myths. Whatever we may think about their bravery, valor, and commitment, the stark reality is that the interests of the men most credited with envisioning Texas and bringing it into being were most often antithetical to the interests of people of color who occupied the same space and time with them. To have Blacks, in particular, acting in concert with White Texians to create a republic in which African-American–based chattel slavery would be protected forever, and in which free Blacks would not be allowed to live, is a bit too much.

It's not unlike the search for Black Confederates, insisting that enslaved people forced into encampments, and into the thick of battle by their enslavers, were full-fledged Confederate soldiers supporting the Lost Cause. The quixotic effort appears designed to satisfy modern-day needs. In an interesting, though admittedly perverse, way, these kinds of efforts can be seen as evidence of some form of progress. People want the individuals from the past they admire to be "right" on the question of race—no matter how wrong they actually were—so that admiring such people poses no problem. The difficulty is that not many European-Americans in the eighteenth and nineteenth centuries were what we would consider to be "right" on the question of race, which, at a minimum, requires believing in the equal humanity of African Americans.

What does this mean for Black Texans thinking of the Texas of the past? Being a historian trying to think and write effectively about the American founding, a period in which Black people were living under oppression at the hands of people who did some other things I admire, requires a degree of detachment. I realize that others may take a different tack. Thinking of past events, and people who lived long ago, and observing the process of change over time satisfies my deep interest in the past on its own terms, though I am also interested in the legacies of the past. I don't feel hostage to others' conceptions of what Texas should mean to me, or accept that Texas "belongs" exclusively to any group of people who lived, or live, there. Being a Black person and a Texan, then, are not in opposition.

6

On Juneteenth

I can't listen to the song "Galveston" without thinking about my great-grandparents on my mother's side. That wasn't always true. When I first heard Glen Campbell's version of the song in 1969, I liked it immediately—the plaintive tone, Campbell's guitar, Jimmy Webb's wistful and poignant lyrics about a young man, a soldier in Vietnam thinking about his hometown and the young girl he left behind. There would have been no obvious reason for me to have connected the story told in that record to my great-grandparents, an African-American couple living on a cotton farm outside of Moscow, Texas, during the first two decades of the twentieth century. One of the tests of a great song or poem—any work of art, really—is its capacity to touch different people in different ways across time. That is a cliché, but like all clichés, it contains a basic truth.

My great-grandfather died before I was born. My great-grandmother lived until I was eleven. Though she was sharp-minded up until she drew her final breath, I was too young to see her as the immensely valuable resource she was. She could have told me about her life in Texas from the final two decades of the nineteenth century and into the twentieth—that would have been the very expression of "change over time," the heart of a historian's work. And what she could have told me about the things she had learned from her mother, who had been born in Mississippi, and likely came to Texas some time in the 1860s! Her mother's father, who was of English extraction, owned her and her mother. Either before or after they arrived in Texas, he freed her when she was very young, possibly still an infant. I've grown up to be a historian of slavery, studying the lives of other families through their family stories. I would love to have learned more from my great-grandmother about some of my own family's experiences.

I would also like to have learned more about the everyday life of my great-grandfather, of which I know only snippets—that his daughters called him "Papa," that, according to his niece, his mother looked like "an old Irish woman" (I don't know what that means), that my great-grandmother used to get up before dawn and prepare huge breakfasts that sounded to me more like lunches or dinners. Planting, ploughing, and picking cotton required many calories, and the pork chops, corn bread, and, sometimes, chicken provided much-needed sustenance. My great-grandfather, along with my great-grandmother, were devout Methodists, and their home was the place visiting ministers stayed when they came to preach at the local church.

Because my paternal grandmother died when my father was eleven, and his father died the year before I was born, I had no contact with an older generation from that line to even overhear their talk about times past, let alone ask them about those days. Acquaintances described my paternal grandfather as having had a very dry sense of humor, and my paternal grandmother as very nice and reserved. I know my father's great-grandfather and his brothers, after slavery ended, saved money and in time bought a fairly large amount of land. They, being very tall and big men, made their living felling trees and preparing them for processing and sale—essentially being lumberjacks. That lasted into my father's time, but just one day working on their land when he was a teenager told my father that this hard life was not for him.

Fortunately, merely being in the presence of my grandmother and her sister so often allowed me to learn the broad contours of their lives growing up on a cotton farm with their parents. I learned that my great-grandfather, during some period of the family's lives, would leave home on a seasonal basis and travel to Galveston to work on the wharves. My great-grandparents had three daughters. Their two sons did not survive. To help my great-grandmother and the girls— my grandmother was in the middle—two young men were hired to live on the farm and help out while he was away. Hence my association of the song "Galveston" with my great-grandparents, although the roles were reversed—the man was in Galveston, the woman at her home. I cannot know for certain that my great-grandfather was thinking plaintively and wistfully about my great-grandmother and his daughters, as the young soldier thought of the young woman in his life, though I like to think so. From all I know of them, the family was devoted to one another. It must have been hard, particularly for the girls, to have their father gone for months at a time. But it was for the good of the family.

Why did he go to Galveston? The island, about 140 miles away from the location of his farm, has connections to people of African descent that go back centuries. I doubt that my great-grandfather, though he was literate, knew of or cared anything about Estebanico, who came ashore at, or in the vicinity of, Galveston in the 1500s as likely the first Black person to set foot in the area that would become Texas. That is an interesting detail for a historian but would have no bearing on a decision to go work there. I am certain my great-grandfather would have known of Galveston's other, more important, historical connections to Black people, for those had more immediate relevance to his life.

On June 19, 1865, as relayed at the beginning of this volume, Gordon Granger, a general in the Army of the United States of America, arrived in Galveston from his post in Louisiana to take command of all the troops in the American army in Texas. The Civil War had been over since April, when the Army of Northern Virginia, headed by General Robert E. Lee, surrendered to General Ulysses S. Grant, commanding general of the Army of the United States. Confederate soldiers in Texas, nevertheless, continued to fight on into May. Indeed, they were victorious in the last battle that took place on Texas soil on May 13, the Battle of Palmito Ranch, near Brownsville, Texas. When it became clear that all other Confederate armies had essentially collapsed—their soldiers were deserting in large numbers—on June 2, 1865, General Kirby Smith, who commanded the Confederate Army of the Trans-Mississippi, surrendered in Galveston to the Army of the United States of America. Texas had become a land in turmoil. Angry Confederate soldiers lashed out after their defeat. Some engaged in rioting and looting. Granger's job was to get to the state, geographically the largest in the Union, impose some degree of order, and announce that all enslaved people were free. He, along with his staff, took up residence in a villa in Galveston. How Granger made the general order known throughout Galveston is disputed. Many histories have Granger reading the Order from the balcony of his quarters. Other accounts say that Granger and soldiers went to strategic places throughout the city and read the Order. In whatever way the news was disseminated, General Order No. 3 had a powerful effect in Texas.

The people of Texas are informed that, in accordance with a proclamation from the Executive of the United States, all slaves are free. This involves an absolute equality of personal rights and rights of property between former masters and slaves, and the connection heretofore existing between them becomes that between employer and hired labor. The freedmen are advised to remain at their present homes and work for wages. They are informed that they will not be allowed to collect at military posts and that they will not be supported in idleness either there or elsewhere.

This Order was based on the Emancipation Proclamation that President Abraham Lincoln, who had been assassinated the previous April, had issued on New Year's Day, 1863. The Thirteenth Amendment, still in the process of being ratified, provided no basis for it.

Some African Americans in Galveston, and likely other residents, already knew the gist of the general order prior to June 19. Galveston, the largest city in Texas, was a port through which most of the cotton picked and processed in the state was shipped out to the world. Port cities are perfect vehicles for transmission of information to people of all degrees of literacy. Two days before General Granger arrived on the island, Black men working on the wharves began to shout in exaltation. When asked what they were celebrating, they replied, because they were free. The news spread to other towns, but the former slaves had to be very wary of open celebration. While the holiday Juneteenth has grown to be an integral part of life in Texas, celebrated now by Blacks and Whites—and appears on its way to becoming a national holiday—Whites in Texas were incensed by what had transpired, so much so that some reacted violently to Blacks' displays of joy at emancipation. In one town, dozens of newly freed enslaved people were whipped for celebrating. All over the South, but in Texas particularly, Whites unleashed a torrent of violence against the freed men and women—and sometimes, the whites who supported them—that lasted for years.

The language of General Order No. 3 not only announced the end of slavery; it used a concept familiar to Americans from the very beginning, though as we know, it was not carried forward. After stating "all slaves are free," the order continues: "This involves an absolute equality of personal rights and rights of property between former masters and slaves." Language about equality echoed the words of the American Declaration of Independence, "all men are created equal." People have long quibbled about what those words meant to Jefferson personally, as if that actually matters to whether the words are true or not. It does not. But Confederates had explicitly rejected the concept of equality announced in the Declaration, as the vice president of the Confederacy, Alexander Stephens, made clear in March 1861 in his infamous "Cornerstone Speech."

The new constitution has put at rest, forever, all the agitating questions relating to our peculiar institution African slavery as it exists amongst us the proper status of the negro in our form of civilization. This was the immediate cause of the late rupture and present revolution. Jefferson in his forecast, had anticipated this, as the "rock upon which the old Union would split." He was right. What was conjecture with him, is now a realized fact. But whether he fully comprehended the great truth upon which that rock stood and stands, may be doubted.

Interestingly, this passage concedes that the Framer's compromise over slavery had left matters unclear enough to be the source of "agitating questions." That uncertainty was caused, in part, by the way some members of the founding generation viewed the institution of slavery and people of African descent.

The prevailing ideas entertained by him [Jefferson] and most of the leading statesmen at the time of the formation of the old constitution, were that the enslavement of the African was in violation of the laws of nature; that it was wrong in principle, socially, morally, and politically. It was an evil they knew not well how to deal with, but the general opinion of the men of that day was that, somehow or other in the order of Prov-

idence, the institution would be evanescent and pass
away. . . .

The Framers could reach a compromise over slavery, and
allow for the formation of the American Union because
Providence, in the form of progress, would solve the
problem.

> Those ideas, however, were fundamentally wrong. They
> rested upon the assumption of the equality of races.
> This was an error. It was a sandy foundation, and the
> government built upon it fell when the "storm came
> and the wind blew." Our new government is founded
> upon exactly the opposite idea; its foundations are
> laid, its corner-stone rests, upon the great truth that
> the negro is not equal to the white man; that slavery
> subordination to the superior race is his natural and
> normal condition. This, our new government, is the
> first, in the history of the world, based upon this great
> physical, philosophical, and moral truth. . . .

That is the basis upon which Texas and other members of the Confederacy had formulated their society. Even
before the war, Texas had made this a part of its creed in its
own Declaration of Independence that formed the Texas
Republic. While it copied the form of the American Declaration, as noted, it left out the language of equality. The

general order announced a state of affairs that completely contravened the racial and economic ideals of the Confederacy. Announcing the end of slavery would have been shocking enough. Stating that the former enslaved would now live in Texas on an equal plane of humanity with whites was on a different order of magnitude of shocking. Had the Order said, "Slavery is over. And former slaves will now become the equivalent of peons on the land of whites, with severely diminished to nonexistent legal, social, and political rights"—the state eventually imposed in Texas and throughout the South—the reaction may have been different. But this Order portended much more than that, as Granger's biographer notes.

It was not just the reaction of White Texans that mattered. The idea that the society that oppressed them might be transformed into one based upon equality influenced Black Texans in much the same way that the Declaration of Independence influenced Blacks in the early American Republic. The fear of the Black imagination was strong all throughout slavery. That was one of the reasons free African Americans posed such a problem and was one of the reasons the Texas Constitution prevented the immigration of free Black people into the republic. Seeing that Black people could exist outside of legal slavery put the lie to the idea that Blacks were born to be slaves. Making life as hard as possible for free African Americans, impairing their movement and economic prospects—even if that meant the state would forgo the economic benefits of talented people who wanted to work—was designed to prove that Blacks could not operate outside of slavery.

Race relations entered a new phase a month after Granger departed Galveston in August. Two months after General Order No. 3 was created, the federal agency set up to help the newly freed people in the wake of the change in their status, the Freedmen's Bureau, opened its Texas branch in Galveston. Conceived as part of the United States Army, General Oliver Howard was made commissioner of the Bureau. Howard, the Maine career soldier who would go on to found and serve as the first president of Howard University, appointed Brigadier General Edgar M. Gregory, a New Yorker, as an assistant commissioner to head the Texas branch. Gregory walked into an almost impossible situation. Texas was so large, and violence against the freedmen and hostility toward the American army so great, that it would have taken a far larger number than the men allotted to the Bureau to effectively carry out its mission. By most accounts, Gregory did the best he could for the newly freed African Americans, but he incurred the wrath of Whites for doing so.

Much has been written about the Freedmen's Bureau, a good deal of it falling in line with the Dunning School view of Reconstruction, which condemned as radical and overreaching the idea that freed Blacks should have been treated as if the words about "equality" actually meant something. William A. Dunning, a historian at Columbia University at the turn of the twentieth century, and his followers, praised the efforts to put White southerners back in control of society. It is difficult to read the historiography, old newspaper entries, and letters, and see historians and other observers portray what was happening in this era, the seeming instinctive sympathy for the lost world of White Texans, the intimations of Black inferiority, while presenting an ostensibly neutral and factual narrative. There is no question that the Bureau did not always make the right choices, and that the men who ran it sometimes fell short of the standards of the racial sensibilities of the late twentieth and early twenty-first centuries. For the most part, however, Gregory and other assistant commissioners, with the discipline of soldiers, tried to uphold the Bureau's mandate. They did so in the presence of a hostile group of people who had lost a war and were implacably opposed to the transformation of their economic and social lives, which had been built on chattel slavery.

General Howard, heading a new bureau that was underfunded and poorly staffed, found Texas the most difficult of all the regions under the Bureau's jurisdiction, its White citizens the most resistant to efforts to effect changes in the position of Blacks in the state. Why would White Texans be more obstreperous than other White southerners? It has been suggested that this was because, unlike other Southern states, Texas had not been defeated militarily. They had won the last battle of the Civil War. That the state had been its own Republic, within the living memory of many Texans, also set them apart from the other Confederates. The very thing that has been seen as a source of strength and pride for latter-day Texans, may have fueled a stubbornness that prevented the state from moving ahead at this crucial moment.

One of the Bureau's most important jobs was supervising the contracts of Black workers. Despite General Order No. 3, some enslavers continued to hold Blacks in slavery; making them work for no pay on threats of violence. These were the kinds of situations the Bureau was designed, in part, to fix. Gregory noted, with seeming surprise, that black Texans, in the face of this hostility, went about the business of making new lives in the state, when they could have, in some places, unleashed carnage on their former enslavers. They, like freed people throughout the South, focused on other things: solemnizing their marriages keeping away from the violence of Whites, trying to reunite with family members who had been sold during slavery, working, and, very happily, taking advantage of the schools the Bureau created. Adults sat in classrooms with children, all eager to learn to read and write. In the midst of all this, any false step by a Black person, any wrong decision by the Bureau—and there definitely were some—was taken as proof that the whole effort was a grievous mistake.

The overall failure of Reconstruction to fulfill the

promise of a South remade with Black southerners participating as equal citizens in the region is well known.
But positive things did happen, particularly the building
of schools to educate freed Blacks. It was from that area
that one of the most influential people in the history of
Blacks in Galveston, and in Texas, appeared. His efforts
laid the groundwork for my great-grandfather's time in the
city. George Ruby, a native New Yorker, who had had an
adventuresome life, was put in charge of the Freedmen's
Bureau school system. He left that position for a stint as
a traveling agent for the Bureau, and returned to Galveston to become a deputy director of customs in 1869. This
was before the end of Reconstruction in Texas in 1870, and
Blacks were voting and holding office across the state. My
own maternal great-great-grandfather registered to vote in
1867. Most important to his career, Ruby became a part of
the Union League, an organization started to support the
candidacy of Abraham Lincoln. The group helped organize
the Republican Party in Texas and sought Black support by
championing the rights of Blacks, to the consternation of
Whites. His involvement with the League helped him be
elected to the Texas State Senate. He also helped organize
the Labor Union of Colored Men to get jobs for Black men
on Galveston's wharves and to help them keep those jobs.

As his influence waned with the weakening of the
Republican Party in Texas, Ruby returned to Louisiana,
where he had lived and worked before coming to Texas.

He believed that prospects for Blacks were better in that state. Fortunately, he had been a mentor to another Black man, this time a native Texan, who took his place in Galveston politics: Norris Wright Cuney. Cuney was the son of Philip Minor Cuney, a very wealthy White planter and state senator who enslaved over one hundred people on his 2,000-acre plantation. With one of those enslaved people, Adeline Stuart, Cuney had eight children. He eventually freed all of them. The younger Cuney became the head of the Union League in Galveston and was influential in Republican Party politics, though he was never able to win higher-level elective office. While he continued his support for Blacks who worked on the wharves at Galveston, keeping alive a tradition that lasted well into the twentieth century, he angered many of them on occasion when he failed to give sufficient support to strikers. Overall, even as Blacks lost power late in the century, having a person like Cuney in place at least provided a visible reminder that people of color could wield power and influence.

Both Ruby and Cuney were dead before the event that transformed Galveston Island in 1901, the catastrophic hurricane that killed as many as 12,000 people and is still considered the worst natural disaster in the history of the United States. The city was determined to rebuild quickly after the destruction. It did so, in part, by inviting large numbers of immigrants to come to work in the city. In sum, Galveston was, for Texas, progressive and cosmopolitan.

Blacks on the island were enormously self-assured, which Whites translated into being "insolent" and "impudent." It was the birthplace of Jack Johnson. I wonder what my great-grandfather made of the place. It would have been enormously different from the society in and around Moscow, deep in East Texas, where one could expect that the traditions and mores laid down in slavery, enforced by the threat and use of vigilante actions, would hold sway. If the promise of Juneteenth lived anywhere in Texas, it was in Galveston.

That sense of promise spread across the state. Black Texans were determined, despite the early intimidating anger of Whites, to celebrate what was initially called Emancipation Day. Most of the first celebrations were in churches, in keeping with the culture of a generally religious people. I also wonder if holding meetings in churches was thought to provide some level of protection in those days. Later, in larger towns, the celebrations migrated to public spaces, though some sort of religious observance might be included in the program. In 1872, in Houston, four Black men, Richard Allen, Richard Brock, Elias Dibble, and Jack Yates, pooled their resources and raised money to buy land in the city for the express purpose of celebrating the holiday, creating Emancipation Park, one of the oldest parks in Texas. It was later taken over by the City of Houston, and in those days of segregation, it was a park for Blacks. Enthusiasm for the celebrations held there, which consisted of speeches, singing, music, waxed and waned over the years, but in the twenty-first century, the renewed interest in Juneteenth spurred the park's revival.

My family went to Houston's Emancipation Park only once, as I recall. All other Juneteenth celebrations were either at my home or at my grandparents' home. The day appeared to me as the first part of a one-two summer punch, June 19 followed closely by July 4—the holiday expressly for Black Texans and the other holiday for all Americans. As far as I knew, Whites did not celebrate Juneteenth during my childhood. But everyone in my area celebrated the Fourth. I do know of the tradition of Blacks celebrating July 5, as a protest to remind people that the ideals of July 4 had not been realized. And I cannot say with any certainty how the people in my family and community viewed the Fourth as a substantive matter—what it was about, how it related to them. It was a holiday, however, a day off to be with relatives and friends. What was not to like? Juneteenth was different. For my great-grandmother, my grandparents, and relatives in their generation, this was the celebration of the freedom of people they had actually known. My great-grandmother's mother had been married three times, out-living all of her husbands. Her last one had been enslaved until the end of the Civil War.

Slavery was just a blink of an eye away from the years my grandparents and their friends were born. Although I was angered by the stories I heard about their lives under Jim Crow, and I had my own issues about the treatment of

Blacks in my lifetime, they surely compared life as it was, knowing what it could have been but for the Civil War, the Emancipation Proclamation, and General Order No. 3. Although there was a very long way to go before we had full and equal citizenship, we were able to gather together as a family to celebrate. Family members who were lost, were lost to death, in the way that all families lose people. No one was being sold away.

We children celebrated with the fireworks my grand-father bought—setting off firecrackers and sparklers well into the night. The traditional Juneteenth menu, in addi-tion to usual southern-style cuisine, included red "soda water," as we called it, and barbecued goat. It was a day of excess for me and my friends on the soda water front. Soda was not a part of our daily experience. It was more like a treat. Besides playing in my grandparents' front and back yards, lighting and throwing firecrackers, we spent the day pulling cans and bottles of soda out of large tin buckets filled with ice. I'm not sure why or how the tradition of eat-ing goat started, as it was not common fare in Texas, as far as I knew. Our family, indeed, skipped eating the goat. My mother's stepfather had a small barbecuing business. People would bring meats to him to prepare, and he spent the day before, and a good part of the day of, the holiday fulfilling orders, some of which, undoubtedly, included goat.

As the years passed, another item was added to the menu. My grandmother, who, by the time I knew her, was a housewife, had her own items to make and sell during the holiday: hot tamales. She made them to order throughout the year to raise money to build a new St. Luke's Methodist United Church, where I had been baptized and where I went as a four-year-old to Miss Ollie's Nursery School, as had my mother. Holidays, Juneteenth included, brought in very large orders. I spent much more time than I wanted in those days sitting with my grandmother, her sister, and my mother, at the kitchen counter and table, preparing dozens of tamales to satisfy her customers and, frankly, to be consumed by our family.

Softening the corn husks in hot water, grinding the pork, beef, or chicken, preparing the masa dough to be spread on the husks, filling the dough with the seasoned meats, and tying the tamales for final preparation—was time-consuming. But it was time spent with people I loved, and who are no longer with me. Like my failure to appreciate what it meant to have a great-grandmother to ask about the past, I didn't know the true value of those moments with the women of my family. Those hours seemed endless to me as a child, but they were actually fleeting. This ritual was fitting, and so very Texan. People of African descent, and to be honest, of some European descent, celebrating the end of slavery in Texas with dishes learned in slavery and a dish favored by ancient Mesoamerican Indians that connected Texas to its Mexican past; so much Texas history brought together for this one special day.

CODA

The reader might ask, after all of this, what it is that I love about the state of Texas? Having questioned the value of love based on legend and myth, how should I feel about the history that is left? This brief sketch of the history of Texas told through vignettes of my family calls to mind something I've often written and said about Jefferson's musings in *Notes on the State of Virginia* on African Americans' prospects in the United States, and what he wrote in his will about the five men he freed. Jefferson wrote in *Notes* that an enslaved person (which, because of the racially based nature of slavery in the country, meant a Black person) could not love the country in which he or she lived. How could they love a country that did not love them, as evidenced by the way the country had treated them? Therefore, Blacks would be happier in some other place, their own country, free from the racial strife that he couldn't see as anything other than inevitable.

In his will, freeing the five men, however, Jefferson petitioned the legislature of Virginia to allow them to remain in the state. He had to do this because, according to Virginia law, an enslaved person who did not get permission to remain in Virginia within a year after emancipation, could be sold back into slavery. When explaining why these men should be allowed to stay, Jefferson said, because Virginia was where "their families and connections" were. At the level of theorizing about nations and countries, it was easy to speak in the abstract—the slave, the country. When dealing with the lives of actual, known people that mattered to him, the focus became sharp and clear.

Abstract notions of the United States, of Virginia—of Texas—for me at least, don't capture why places are worthy of love. When asked, as I have been very often, to explain what I love about Texas, given all that I know of what has happened there—and is still happening there—the best response I can give is that this is where my first family and connections were. It's where I lived with my mother, my father, and brothers. It's where I rode back and forth between Conroe and Livingston to visit my grandparents, aunts, and cousins. It's where my father drove me thirty-five miles to Huntsville, at my mother's behest, for piano lessons with Mrs. Tull, who had been a professional classical pianist. *What was my mother thinking was going to happen with that!?* In other words, Texas is where my mother's boundless dreams for me took flight. It's also where I learned to think that people could, and should, try, in whatever way they can, to make life better for others alive today and for those to come. That this feeling—this thought—came to me in a place that was at once so very difficult, so full of good things, and so full of potential, shaped my thinking and actions in important ways.

About the difficulties of Texas: Love does not require taking an uncritical stance toward the object of one's affections. In truth, it often requires the opposite. We can't be of real service to the hopes we have for places—and people, ourselves included—without a clear-eyed assessment of their (and our) strengths and weaknesses. That often demands a willingness to be critical, sometimes deeply so. How that is done matters, of course. Striking the right balance can be exceedingly hard.

I hope I've achieved the proper equilibrium.

ACKNOWLEDGMENTS

This book grew out of a continuing conversation I've had with my editor, Bob Weil, who has encouraged me over the years to write about Texas. I'm deeply grateful for his support, and that of our friend—and my agent—Faith Childs. A number of my friends and colleagues offered helpful suggestions. My frequent collaborator Peters S. Onuf and my former New York Law School colleague David S. Schoenbrod graciously read the whole manuscript. Andres Resendez, James Goodman, Tiya Miles, Philip Deloria, Barry Bienstock, Andrew Torget, and Martha Minow read select chapters. I benefited enormously from their insights.

As always, I thank my husband, Robert R. Reed, for his enthusiasm and steadfast support. This book was written during the summer of 2020 when we Manhattanites were in lockdown due to the COVID-19 pandemic. The best part of that harrowing period was getting to spend all of those days with him.

BOOKS AND
ARTICLES CONSULTED

PREFACE

Olivia B. Waxman, "Activists Are Pushing to Make Juneteenth a National Holiday. Here's the History Behind Their Fight," *Time*, June 17, 2020, https://time.com/5853800/juneteenth-national-holiday/.

CHAPTER ONE: "THIS, THEN, IS TEXAS"

"Big Thicket," http://houstonwilderness.org/big-thicket.
Andrew J. Torget, *Seeds of Empire: Cotton, Slavery, and the Transformation of the Texas Borderlands, 1800–1850* (Chapel Hill, NC, 2015).

CHAPTER TWO: A TEXAS TOWN

Bishop Michael Rinehart, "Lynchings in Conroe," https://tlgcconnections.wordpress.com/2019/04/27/lynchings-in-conroe/.
Nick Davies, "The Deadly Secrets of a Small Town in Texas," *The Guardian*, February 2, 1991, https://www.nickdavies.net/1991/02/02/the-deadly-secrets-of-a-small-town-in-texas/.
Nick Davies, "The Town That Loved Lynching," *The Scotsman and the New Zealand Dominion*, April 10, 1989.
"Murder in the Courtroom," https://hauntedconroe.com/murder-in-the-courtroom/.
White v. Texas, 310 U.S. 530 (1940).

CHAPTER THREE:
ORIGIN STORIES: AFRICANS IN TEXAS

Ira Berlin, *Many Thousands Gone: The First Two Centuries of Slavery in North America* (Cambridge, MA, 1998).

Ira Berlin, *Generation of Captivity: A History of African-American Slaves* (Cambridge, MA, 2004).

Andrés Reséndez, *A Land So Strange: The Epic Journey of Cabeza de Vaca: The Extraordinary Tale of a Shipwrecked Spaniard Who Walked Across America in the Sixteenth Century* (New York, 2007).

Donald Chipman, "Estevanico," https://www.tshaonline.org/handbook/entries/estevanico.

Nicqel Terry Ellis, "Forget What You Know About 1619, Historians Say, Slavery Began a Century Before Jamestown," https://www.staugustine.com/news/20191219/forget-what-you-know-about-1619-historians-say-slavery-began-half-century-before-jamestown-in-st-augustine.

Library of Congress, "The Limitations of the Slave Narrative Collection," https://www.loc.gov/collections/slave-narratives-from-the-federal-writers-project-1936-to-1938/articles-and-essays/introduction-to-the-wpa-slave-narratives/limitations-of-the-slave-narrative-collection/.

CHAPTER FOUR:
PEOPLE OF THE PAST AND THE PRESENT

Pekka Hamalainen, *The Comanche Empire* (New Haven, CT, 2008).

Paul H. Carlson and Tom Crum, *Myth, Memory, and Massacre: The Pease River Capture of Cynthia Parker* (Lubbock, TX, 2010).

Martha L. Finch, *Dissenting Bodies: Corporealities in Early New England* (New York, 2009).

Stephen Harrigan, *Big Wonderful Thing: A History of Texas* (Austin, 2019).

Sheri Marie Shuck-Hall, *Journey to the West: The Alabama & Coushatta Indians* (Norman, OK, 2008).

"Alibates Flint Quarries and Ruins," https://www.texasbeyondhistory.net/alibates/.

CHAPTER FIVE: REMEMBER THE ALAMO

William C. Davis, *Three Roads to the Alamo* (New York, 1998).

Stephan L. Hardin, *Texian Illiad: A Military History of the Texas Revolution 1835–1836* (Austin, 1994).

Randolph B. Campbell, *An Empire for Slavery: The Peculiar Institution in Texas, 1821–1865* (Baton Rouge, LA, 1991).

Pete A. Y. Gunter, *The Big Thicket: An Ecological Reevaluation* (Denton, TX, 1993).

Jeffrey D. Dunn and James Lutzweiler, "Yellow Rose of Texas," https://www.tshaonline.org/handbook/entries/yellow-rose-of-texas.

Stephen Harrigan, "Texas Primer: The Yellow Rose of Texas," *Texas Monthly*, April 1984,

https://www.texasmonthly.com/the-culture/texas-primer-the-yellow-rose-of-texas/.

Logan Hawkes, "The Uncertain History of Emily West," http://texaslesstraveled.com/emilyessay.htm.

Amelia White, "Who Was the Yellow Rose of Texas? Myths and Legends of the Texas Revolution," https://medium.com/@OfficialAlamo/who-was-the-yellow-rose-of-texas-750c95617241.

CHAPTER SIX: ON JUNETEENTH

Gary Cartwright, *Galveston: A History of the Island* (New York, 1991).

Robert C. Conner, *General Gordon Granger: The Savior of Chickamauga and the Man Behind "Juneteenth"* (Philadelphia and Oxford, 2013).

Barry A. Crouch, *The Freedmen's Bureau and Black Texans* (Austin, 1992).

Eric Foner, *Reconstruction: America's Unfinished Revolution* (New York, 1998).

Karl Jacoby, *The Strange Career of William Ellis: The Texas Slave Who Became a Millionaire* (New York, 2016).

David G. McComb, *Galveston: A History* (Austin, 1986).

Jack Healy, "Black, and Bent on His Native American Rights," *New York Times*, September 8, 2020.

Teresa Palomo Acosta, "Juneteenth," https://www.tshaonline.org/handbook/entries/juneteenth.

Gregg Andrews, "Black Working-Class Political Activism and Biracial Unionism: Galveston Longshoremen in Jim Crow Texas, 1919–1921," *Journal of Southern History* 74, no. 3 (August 2008): 627–668.

Ed Cotham, "Juneteenth: Four Myths and One Great Truth," *Daily News* (Galveston County), June 18, 2014.

Cecil Harper, Jr., "Freedman's Bureau," https://www.tshaonline.org/handbook/entries/freedmens-bureau.

"Emancipation Park," https://www.houstontx.gov/parks/parksites/emancipationpark.html.

Merline Pitre, "Cuney, Norris Wright (1846–1898)," https://www.tshaonline
.org/handbook/entries/cuney-norris-wright.

Merline Pitre, "Ruby, George Thompson (1841–1882)," https://www.tshaonline
.org/handbook/entries/ruby-george-thompson.

James V. Reese, "The Early History of Labor Organizations in Texas, 1838–
1876," *Southwestern Historical Quarterly* 72, no. 1 (July 1968): 1–20.

ABOUT THE AUTHOR

Annette Gordon-Reed is the author of the National Book Award– and Pulitzer Prize–winning *The Hemingses of Monticello: An American Family* and is the Carl M. Loeb University Professor at Harvard University.